Internet Law Series

Jurisdiction

Jonathan L. Zittrain
Oxford Internet Institute
Harvard Law School

FOUNDATION PRESS
NEW YORK, NEW YORK
2005

The image on the cover and title-page is of the Principality of Sealand, with permission: http://www.offshore–radio.de/fleet/sealand.htm.

The principality of Sealand is a micronation that claims to be an independent sovereign principality, though it is not officially recognized as such by any member of the United Nations. If considered as a country, it is by far the smallest one on earth: it has a population that rarely exceeds five, and an inhabitable area of some 550 m².

Sealand occupies a structure that was created when a purpose–built World War II–era Royal Navy barge was towed to a position above Rough Sands sandbar in the North North Sea and had its hold intentionally flooded. It is sited six statute miles (10 km) off the coast of Suffolk, England, at 51° 53' 40" N 1° 28' 57" E and has been occupied since 1967 by the family of Paddy Roy Bates and their associates.

(From the Wikipedia, http://en.wikipedia.org/wiki/Sealand)

Book editing, layout, and cover design: Amy Whitaker

© 2005 By FOUNDATION PRESS
        395 Hudson Street
        New York, NY 10014
        Phone Toll Free 1–877–888–1330
        Fax (212) 367–6799
        fdpress.com
Printed in the United States of America

ISBN 1–58778–979–5

 *TEXT IS PRINTED ON 10% POST CONSUMER RECYCLED PAPER*

ACKNOWLEDGEMENTS

Harvard Law School provided support through multiple iterations of its Summer Research Program to enable me to draft this and other Internet Law Series modules. I thank David Buchwald, Bryan Choi, John Fiore, Aaron Kaufman, Megan Kirk, Adam Lawton, Isaac Lidsky, and K. Joon Oh, for excellent research assistance, Steve Errick at Foundation Press forcontinuing encouragement, my Internet Law Casebook co–authors Yochai Benkler, Terry Fisher, Charlie Nesson, and Larry Lessig for many discussions and inspirations, Diane Long for production coordination and assistance, and Amy Whitaker for design and management genius.

In addition, I would like to acknowledge the authors and original publishers of various works reprinted in this volume:

Barlow, John Perry, "Declaration of Independence in Cyberspace," 1996. With permission of the author.

Garfinkel, Simson, "Welcome to Sealand, Now Bugger Off," *Wired,* July 2000. With permission of the author. Originally published in *Wired.*

Helfer, Laurence R. and Graeme B. Dinwoodie, Designing Non–National Systems: The Case of the Uniform Domain Name Dispute Resolution Policy, 43 WM AND MARY L. REV. 141 (October 2001). © 2000 *William and Mary Law Review,* and with permission of the authors.

Johnson, David R. and David G. Post, "Law and Borders: The Rise of Law in Cyberspace," 48 STAN. L. REV. 1367 (1996). © 1996 David R. Johnson and David G. Post. Available at http://www.cli.org-/X0025_LBFIN.html. Permission granted to redistribute freely, in whole or in part,with this notice attached.

Lessig, Lawrence, "The Zones of Cyberspace," 48 STAN. L. REV. 1403 (1996). With permission of the *Stanford Law Review.*

Quova, Inc., "Company Fact Sheet," http://www.quova.com/company/quova–factsheet.shtml, June 2005. With permission of Quova, Inc.

Price, Monroe E., "The Newness of New Technology," 22 CARDOZO L. REV. 1885 (2001). With permission of the author.

Reidenberg, Joel R., "Democracy and the Internet," 42 JURIMETRICS J. 261 (2002). With permission of the author.

Thornburg, Elizabeth G., "Fast, Cheap and Out of Control: Lessons from the ICANN Dispute Resolution Process," 6 J. SMALL & EMERGING BUS. L. 191 (2002). With permission of the *Lewis and Clark Law Review* and the author.

Zittrain, Jonathan L., "Be Careful What You Ask For: Reconciling a Global Internet and a Local Law," *Who Rules the Net?,* Cato Institute, 2003. With permission of the Cato Institute and the author.

Jonathan Zittrain
July 2005

TABLE OF CONTENTS

John Perry Barlow is a retired Wyoming cattle rancher, a former lyricist for the Grateful Dead, and a thinker on cyberspace topics. In 1996, not long after the invention of the Web browser, and before broadband Internet connections became available to many residences and schools, he penned "A Declaration of the Independence of Cyberspace" that crystallized the perceived difficulties of regulating the new environment. Many of these difficulties were grounded in a seemingly revolutionary feature of the Net: an undifferentiated global reach, where any part of the world was as good as next door.

A DECLARATION OF THE INDEPENDENCE OF CYBERSPACE
John Perry Barlow
1996

> Governments of the Industrial World, you weary giants of flesh and steel, I come from Cyberspace, the new home of Mind. On behalf of the future, I ask you of the past to leave us alone. You are not welcome among us. You have no sovereignty where we gather.
>
> . . .
>
> Governments derive their just powers from the consent of the governed. You have neither solicited nor received ours. We

did not invite you. You do not know us, nor do you know our world. Cyberspace does not lie within your borders. Do not think that you can build it, as though it were a public construction project. You cannot. It is an act of nature and it grows itself through our collective actions.

You have not engaged in our great and gathering conversation, nor did you create the wealth of our marketplaces. You do not know our culture, our ethics, or the unwritten codes that already provide our society more order than could be obtained by any of your impositions.

You claim there are problems among us that you need to solve. You use this claim as an excuse to invade our precincts. Many of these problems don't exist. Where there are real conflicts, where there are wrongs, we will identify them and address them by our means. We are forming our own Social Contract. This governance will arise according to the conditions of our world, not yours. Our world is different.

. . .

Your legal concepts of property, expression, identity, movement, and context do not apply to us. They are all based on matter, and there is no matter here.

Our identities have no bodies, so, unlike you, we cannot obtain order by physical coercion. We believe that from ethics, enlightened self–interest, and the commonweal, our governance will emerge. Our identities may be distributed across many of your jurisdictions. The only law that all our constituent cultures would generally recognize is the Golden Rule. We hope we will be able to build our particular solutions on that basis. But we cannot accept the solutions you are attempting to impose.

. . .

In our world, all the sentiments and expressions of humanity, from the debasing to the angelic, are parts of a seamless whole, the global conversation of bits. We cannot separate the air that chokes from the air upon which wings beat.

In China, Germany, France, Russia, Singapore, Italy and the United States, you are trying to ward off the virus of liberty by erecting guard posts at the frontiers of Cyberspace. These may keep out the contagion for a small time, but they will not work in a world that will soon be blanketed in bit-bearing media.

Your increasingly obsolete information industries would perpetuate themselves by proposing laws, in America and elsewhere, that claim to own speech itself throughout the world. These laws would declare ideas to be another industrial product, no more noble than pig iron. In our world, whatever the human mind may create can be reproduced and distributed infinitely at no cost. The global conveyance of thought no longer requires your factories to accomplish.

These increasingly hostile and colonial measures place us in the same position as those previous lovers of freedom and self-determination who had to reject the authorities of distant, uninformed powers. We must declare our virtual selves immune to your sovereignty, even as we continue to consent to your rule over our bodies. We will spread ourselves across the Planet so that no one can arrest our thoughts.

We will create a civilization of the Mind in Cyberspace. May it be more humane and fair than the world your governments have made before.

Davos, Switzerland
February 8, 1996

I. AN OVERVIEW OF JURISDICTIONAL PROBLEMS IN CYBERSPACE

As most first–year civil procedure students discover, "jurisdiction" is a term that can mean several distinct things. When invoked by judges and commentators in Internet–related cases, the term has come to have an everything–but–the–kitchen–sink breadth of applications. At its core, jurisdiction is about the boundaries of a sovereign's exercise of its power. What are the constraints on its legal reach, whether internally or externally imposed? To what extent can faraway or otherwise unconnected people and institutions be called to account by the sovereign? Closely related, and often overlapping, questions concern concepts of choice of law—which sovereign's laws should apply to a situation that spans multiple jurisdictions and which physical locations are suitable for the parties to settle their dispute.

The global nature of the Internet—both its global reach and its perceived "boundaryless" architecture—presents a host of jurisdictional complexities for any sovereign seeking to define and enforce laws regulating its use. Unfortunately, discussions of Internet law frequently lump these various concepts indiscriminately under the rubric of "jurisdiction." Conflating these concepts runs the risk of obscuring the relevant doctrine to apply to solve a very specific problem. Equally, doing dry jurisdictional exercises upon a specific set of problems can obscure the fascinatingly complicated and important questions raised by the Internet's challenge to a sovereign's control.

To explore these issues, this text first reviews the basics of jurisdiction as applied to the Internet. Next, it maps out the perceived "boundarylessness" of the Internet and recent technical efforts to circumvent or change this architectural characteristic. Finally, it explores various perspectives on the optimal extent of "local" jurisdiction.

The overview of jurisdiction begins with three areas of conflict: personal jurisdiction, choice of law, and enforcement.

I.A. Personal Jurisdiction

One of the earliest sets of chestnuts about cyberlaw relies on confusions arising from the network–enabled interactions of faraway parties. Judges have struggled, with understandably mixed success, to apply traditional principles and limits of long–arm jurisdiction—and to invoke roughly analogous pre–Internet situations (such as disputes arising from telephone calls) to assist those applications. For example: Here's a sampling of the sorts of problems that commonly arise in cyberlaw under the rubric of personal jurisdiction:

A, in Alabama, sends a threat by e–mail to C, who retrieves the e–mail from America Online's computers in Virginia and reads it on her screen in California. Where has the threat "happened?" Can California authorities prosecute A? Can Virginia?

D, in Delaware, is the victim of allegedly defamatory speech posted by A, in Australia. Should A have to travel to Delaware to defend herself merely for posting information to a personal Web site accessible worldwide? Should D have to travel to Australia to seek redress for harm to his reputation in Delaware?

A, in the city of Abilene, e–mails B, in Boston and offers to purchase his vintage 1973 Slimline Telecaster guitar. B sends an e–mail confirming the deal, but then fails to send the guitar after receiving A's payment. Where was the contract made?

Betty's Beauty Salon, in Boston, feels that its trademark is being infringed by Betty's Beauty Products, a California company whose Web site is available to Boston residents. Can Boston Betty sue Berkeley Betty in federal court in Massachusetts?

These hypothetical situations outline the most basic, if least interesting, questions of Internet jurisdiction. Where does the actual harm in such cases take place? At the point of transmission? At the point where the offending material is received or read? Or perhaps at some (or all) points in between—that is, at any point where a server or router electronically handled or forwarded the material? The typical dilemma for a thoughtful state jurist engaging in a personal jurisdiction calculus is that, on the one hand, harm entering the state ought to be redressable there so jurisdiction should obtain; on the other hand, every state with an Internet connection could perform the same calculus—rendering an intuitively unfair result that a single digital utterance could render its author open to suit virtually everywhere.

I.B. Conflict of Laws and the Convoy Problem

Quite often what is really at stake in an exercise of personal jurisdiction is which sovereign's law will be applied to the activity in question. In other words, many "jurisdiction" cases in cyberlaw are quite settled that personal jurisdiction might be found for plaintiff and defendant; rather, the question at stake is the fairness in having a remote jurisdiction's law applied to a distant defendant's Internet activities, especially when such application could, in essence, require all Internet users in the world to hew to that law. For example:

TotalNews, an Arizona company whose Web servers also were residing in that state, sought to make a profit by linking to and then incorporating news stories from the Web sites of major newspapers into "frames" on its own homepage. Several of these newspapers, feeling that TotalNews was misappropriating their material (particularly since their stories appeared surrounded by the ads on the TotalNews homepage rather than the ads accompanying the original story), sued TotalNews in New York, a state known for its well-developed common law anti-misappropriation doctrine. Supposing personal jurisdiction could be successfully obtained over the defendants in New York (perhaps soley due to their Web contacts with people within the state), is it fair that New York's law alone should determine the global propriety of the TotalNews site? If so, alert plaintiffs might forum–shop to determine where to bring a case, so as to apply the most sympathetic law to their respective causes.

Felix Somm was running CompuServe Germany, a subsidiary of CompuServe, Inc., the U.S.–based parent company. A German state prosecutor brought criminal charges against him for CompuServe's allowing German subscribers to read "newsgroups" carried by CompuServe that were alleged to have pornography that was illegal to transmit to Germany. Somm claimed that there was no way for CompuServe to identify who among its members was coming from Germany. What should CompuServe Germany have been required to do?

Le Tribunal de Grande Instance de Paris issued a preliminary injunction against Yahoo!, Inc., an American company with its Web servers located in the United States, in a case brought against Yahoo! and Yahoo! France by two nonprofit organizations dedicated to eliminating anti–Semitism. In France, the display of objects representing symbols of Nazi ideology was considered a violation of the penal code, and Yahoo!'s auctions featured the sale—and concomitant digital display—of Nazi memorabilia, such as daggers from the Third Reich. If the French authorities were successful in forcing Yahoo! to remove the offending pages from its auction site, of what import would the fact have been that, under U.S. constitutional law, Yahoo! was well within its rights to post the material?

We call this set of issues the "slowest ship in the convoy" problem. Put simply, the potential application of every sovereign's law to Internet activity might force such activity to conform to the most restrictive sets of law, or become entangled in hopelessly conflicting or even outright contradictory demands. This is distinct from the problems of personal jurisdiction. Here, we worry not about the *inconvenience* or *unfairness* of remote or even simultaneous lawsuits launched around the world against a single Web site or other Internet action, but rather about the outcomes of those lawsuits: outcomes ordained by one country, even when other sovereigns might object. Within the United States, the "dormant commerce clause" of the U.S. Constitution is thought to limit such conflicting legal results at the state level—at the price of preventing a given state from being able to control activity clearly having impact within its borders. Internationally, there is no corresponding framework to work through such conflicts.

I.C. Enforcement and Power Issues

Many issues of Internet jurisdiction really turn out to be questions of power over an alleged wrongdoer—not whether personal jurisdiction can be legally obtained, or whether it is fair to apply one's local law to the activity—(an activity perhaps so bad that almost everyone's law would proscribe it)—but rather how one can effectively identify, locate, and prosecute the online offender. Consider the following:

A, in Alabama, has her online bill pay service password compromised, and her money is withdrawn—to Vanuatu. Her long–distance phone calls to the Vanuatuan police go unreturned.

The state of Minnesota decrees it to be illegal for someone to operate a gambling Web site that accepts bets from those located in Minnesota. A gambling Web site is set up in the Cayman Islands, and Minnesotans gamble there. What should the attorney general of Minnesota do?

Walt Disney Co. is not pleased to find that "screwmickeyand-goofy.com" has been registered by a shadowy "anti–Mickey action league" that runs a Web site featuring copyrighted Disney cartoons interspersed with blistering commentary. The domain name directory lists the holder of the domain name as "M. Mouse," living at "123 Mouse Row," and the servers for the site appear to be run from Sealand, a small World War II antiaircraft platform in the North Sea. What can Disney do about it?

In response to the French court decision in the *Yahoo!* case, the French groups sought to prevent Yahoo! from making available in France any Web pages stored on Yahoo!'s servers that auctioned Nazi objects or presented any materials containing Nazi sympathy or Holocaust denial—a possibility that Yahoo! claimed was technologically impossible. Should the United States courts respect any French judgments in the matter, allowing authorities to attach Yahoo! bank accounts in California in order to pay damages awarded by the French court? Could U.S. courts force Yahoo! to remove the offending material, despite its legality under U.S. law?

We encounter here a conflict that, at its heart, represents an issue of technological possibility and, ultimately, raw power.

II. DOCTRINAL APPROACHES TO THE TAXONOMY OF JURISDICTIONAL PROBLEMS

II.A. Personal Jurisdiction

The requirement of personal jurisdiction prevents a sovereign's courts from exercising authority over persons who have little or no relation to that sovereign. Personal jurisdiction is defined as "[a] court's power to bring a person into its adjudicative process." BLACK'S LAW DICTIONARY 870 (8th ed. 2004). It is distinct from subject matter jurisdiction, which governs the types of cases—whether traffic violations, murder trials, or constitutional questions—that a court is competent to decide.

The traditional principles of personal jurisdiction in the United States, expressed in *Pennoyer v. Neff*, 95 U.S. 714, 722 (1877), were based on territorial boundaries: "every State possesses exclusive jurisdiction and sovereignty over persons and property within its territory" and "no State can exercise direct jurisdiction and authority over persons or property without its territory." Since the time of *Pennoyer*, personal jurisdiction doctrine has expanded beyond the strict requirement of physical presence within a territory. In the second half of the twentieth century, contacts with a forum state through the mail, telephone calls, or television broadcasts provided a basis for exercising personal jurisdiction over nonresident defendants. See, *e.g.*, *McGee v. International Life Insurance Co.*, 355 U.S. 220 (1957); *Schlussel v. Schlussel*, 190 Cal. Rptr. 95, (Cal. Ct. App. 1983); *Indianapolis*

Colts v. Metropolitan Baltimore Football Club, 34 F.3d 410 (7th Cir. 1994).

The following case represents a further expansion and reformation of personal jurisdiction principles in the context of Web sites argued at just the time that Barlow drafted his Declaration of Independence. Although the utility of a Web–specific doctrine may be disputed, to whatever extent there is a canon in cyber-law, the widely–cited *Zippo* decision is often the starting point for the jurisdictional analysis.

ZIPPO MANUFACTURING CO. V. ZIPPO DOT COM
952 F. Supp. 1119 (W.D. Pa. 1997)

McLAUGHLIN, J.

This is an Internet domain name dispute. At this stage of the controversy, we must decide the Constitutionally permissible reach of Pennsylvania's Long Arm Statute, 42 Pa.C.S.A. § 5322, through cyberspace. Plaintiff Zippo Manufacturing Corporation ("Manufacturing") has filed a five count complaint against Zippo Dot Com, Inc. ("Dot Com") alleging trademark dilution, infringement, and false designation under the Federal Trademark Act, 15 U.S.C. § § 1051–1127. In addition, the Complaint alleges causes of action based on state law trademark dilution under 54 Pa.C.S.A. § 1124, and seeks equitable accounting and imposition of a constructive trust. Dot Com has moved to dismiss for lack of personal jurisdiction and improper venue pursuant to Fed. R. Civ. P 12(b)(2) and (3) or, in the alternative, to transfer the case pursuant to 28 U.S.C. § 1406(a). For the reasons set forth below, Defendant's motion is denied.

I. BACKGROUND
The facts relevant to this motion are as follows. Manufacturing

is a Pennsylvania corporation with its principal place of business in Bradford, Pennsylvania. Manufacturing makes, among other things, well known "Zippo" tobacco lighters. Dot Com is a California corporation with its principal place of business in Sunnyvale, California. Dot Com operates an Internet Web site and an Internet news service and has obtained the exclusive right to use the domain names "zippo.com," "zippo.net" and "zipponews.com" on the Internet.

What does the court mean here by "exclusive right"? Who granted Dot Com this right?

Dot Com's Web site contains information about the company, advertisements and an application for its Internet news service. The news service itself consists of three levels of membership—public/free, "Original" and "Super." Each successive level offers access to a greater number of Internet newsgroups. A customer who wants to subscribe to either the "Original" or "Super" level of service, fills out an on–line application that asks for a variety of information including the person's name and address. Payment is made by credit card over the Internet or the telephone. The application is then processed and the subscriber is assigned a password which permits the subscriber to view and/or download Internet newsgroup messages that are stored on the Defendant's server in California.

Dot Com's contacts with Pennsylvania have occurred almost exclusively over the Internet. Dot Com's offices, employees and Internet servers are located in California. Dot Com maintains no offices, employees or agents in Pennsylvania. Dot Com's advertising for its service to Pennsylvania residents involves posting information about its service on its Web page, which is accessible to Pennsylvania residents via the Internet. Defendant has approximately 140,000 paying subscribers worldwide. Approximately two percent (3,000) of those subscribers are Pennsylvania residents. These subscribers have contracted to receive Dot Com's service by visiting its Web site and filling out the application. Additionally, Dot Com has entered into agreements with seven Internet access providers in Pennsylvania to permit their subscribers to access Dot Com's news service. Two of these providers are located in the Western District of Pennsylvania.

The basis of the trademark claims is Dot Com's use of the word "Zippo" in the domain names it holds, in numerous locations in its Web site and in the heading of Internet newsgroup messages that have been posted by Dot Com subscribers. . . .

. . .

III. DISCUSSION

A. Personal Jurisdiction

1. The Traditional Framework

Our authority to exercise personal jurisdiction in this case is conferred by state law. Fed. R. Civ. P. 4(e); *Mellon,* 960 F.2d at 1221. The extent to which we may exercise that authority is governed by the Due Process Clause of the Fourteenth Amendment to the Federal Constitution. *Kulko v. California Supreme Court,* 436 U.S. 84, 91, 56 L. Ed. 2d 132, 98 S. Ct. 1690 (1978).

. . .[E]ven if Dot Com's conduct did not satisfy a specific provision of the statute, we would nevertheless be authorized to exercise jurisdiction to the "fullest extent allowed under the Constitution of the United States." 42 Pa.C.S.A. § 5322(b).

The Constitutional limitations on the exercise of personal jurisdiction differ depending upon whether a court seeks to exercise general or specific jurisdiction over a non-resident defendant. *Mellon,* 960 F.2d at 1221. General jurisdiction permits a court to exercise personal jurisdiction over a non-resident defendant for non-forum related activities when the defendant has engaged in "systematic and continuous" activities in the forum state. *Helicopteros Nacionales de Colombia, S.A. v. Hall,* 466 U.S. 408, 414–16 (1984). In the absence of general jurisdiction, specific jurisdiction permits a court to exercise personal jurisdiction over a non-resident defendant for forum–related activities where the "relationship between the defendant and the forum falls within the 'minimum contacts' framework" of *International Shoe Co. v. Washington,* 326 U.S. 310 (1945) and its progeny. *Mellon,* 960 F.2d at 1221. Manufacturing does not contend that we should exercise general personal jurisdiction over Dot Com. Manufacturing concedes that if personal jurisdiction exists in this case, it must be specific.

A three–pronged test has emerged for determining whether the exercise of specific personal jurisdiction over a non–resident defendant is appropriate: (1) the defendant must have sufficient "minimum contacts" with the forum state, (2) the claim asserted against the defendant must arise out of those contacts, and (3) the exercise of jurisdiction must be reasonable. *Id.* The "Constitutional touchstone" of the minimum contacts analysis is embodied in the first prong, "whether the defendant purposefully established" contacts with the forum state. *Burger King Corp. v. Rudzewicz,* 471 U.S. 462, 475 (1985) (citing *International Shoe Co. v. Washington,* 326 U.S. 310, 319 (1945)). Defendants who "'reach out beyond one state' and create continuing relationships and obligations with the citizens of another state are subject to regulation and sanctions in the other State for consequences of their actions." *Id.* . . . . "[T]he foreseeability that is critical to the due process analysis is . . . that the defendant's conduct and connection with the forum State are such that he should reasonably expect to be haled into court there." *World–Wide Volkswagen Corp. v. Woodson,* 444 U.S. 286, 297 (1980). This protects defendants from being forced to answer for their actions in a foreign jurisdiction based on "random, fortuitous or attenuated" contacts. *Keeton v. Hustler Magazine, Inc.,* 465 U.S. 770, 774 (1984). "Jurisdiction is proper, however, where contacts proximately result from actions by the defendant himself that create a 'substantial connection' with the forum State." Burger King, 471 U.S. at 475 (citing *McGee v. International Life Insurance Co.,* 355 U.S. 220, 223 (1957)).

The "reasonableness" prong exists to protect defendants against unfairly inconvenient litigation. *World–Wide Volkswagen*, 444 U.S. at 292. Under this prong, the exercise of jurisdiction will be reasonable if it does not offend "traditional notions of fair play and substantial justice." *International Shoe*, 326 U.S. at 316. When determining the reasonableness of a particular forum, the court must consider the burden on the defendant in light of other factors including: "the forum state's interest in adjudicating the dispute; the plaintiff's interest in obtaining convenient and effective relief, at least when that interest is not adequately protected by the plaintiff's right to choose the forum; the interstate judicial system's interest in obtaining the most efficient resolution of controversies; and the shared interest of the several states in furthering fundamental substantive social policies." World–Wide Volkswagen, 444 U.S. at 292 [ ].

2. *The Internet and Jurisdiction*

In *Hanson v. Denckla*, the Supreme Court noted that "as technological progress has increased the flow of commerce between States, the need for jurisdiction has undergone a similar increase." *Hanson v. Denckla*, 357 U.S. 235, 250–51, 2 L. Ed. 2d 1283, 78 S. Ct. 1228 (1958). Twenty seven years later, the Court observed that jurisdiction could not be avoided "merely because the defendant did not *physically* enter the forum state. *Burger King*, 471 U.S. at 476. The Court observed that:

It is an inescapable fact of modern commercial life that a substantial amount of commercial business is transacted solely by mail and wire communications across state lines, thus obviating the need for physical presence within a State in which business is conducted. *Id.*

Enter the Internet, a global "'super–network' of over 15,000 computer networks used by over 30 million individuals, corporations, organizations, and educational institutions worldwide." *Panavision v. Toeppen,* 938 F. Supp. 616 (S.D.Cal. 1996) (citing *American Civil Liberties Union v. Reno,* 929 F. Supp. 824, 830–48 (E.D.Pa. 1996). "In recent years, businesses have begun to use the Internet to provide information and products to consumers and other businesses." *Id.* The Internet makes it possible to conduct business throughout the world entirely from a desktop. With this global revolution looming on the horizon, the development of the law concerning the permissible scope of personal jurisdiction based on Internet use is in its infant stages. The cases are scant. Nevertheless, our review of the available cases and materials reveals that the likelihood that personal jurisdiction can be constitutionally exercised is directly proportionate to the nature and quality of commercial activity that an entity conducts over the Internet.

Where does nytimes.com fit on this sliding scale?

This sliding scale is consistent with well developed personal jurisdiction principles. At one end of the spectrum are situations where a defendant clearly does business over the Internet. If the defendant enters into contracts with residents of a foreign jurisdiction that involve the knowing and repeated transmission of computer files over the Internet, personal jurisdiction is proper. *E.g., Compuserve, Inc. v. Patterson,* 89 F.3d 1257 (6th Cir. 1996). At the opposite end are situations where a defendant has simply posted information on an Internet Web site which is accessible to users in foreign jurisdictions. A passive Web site that does little more than make information available to those who are interested in it is not grounds for the exercise personal jurisdiction. *E.g., Bensusan Restaurant Corp., v. King,* 937 F. Supp. 295 (S.D.N.Y. 1996). The middle ground is occupied by interactive Web sites where a user can exchange information with the host computer. In these cases, the exercise of jurisdiction is determined by examining the level of interactivity and commercial nature of the exchange of information that occurs on the Web site. *E.g., Maritz, Inc. v. Cybergold, Inc.,* 940 F. Supp. 96, 1996 U.S. Dist. LEXIS 14976 (E.D.Mo. 1996).

. . .

3. *Application to this Case*

First, we note that this is not an Internet advertising case in the line of *Inset Systems* and *Bensusan, supra.* Dot Com has not just posted information on a Web site that is accessible to Pennsylvania residents who are connected to the Internet. This is not even an interactivity case in the line of *Maritz, supra.* Dot Com has done more than create an interactive Web site through which it exchanges information with Pennsylvania residents in hopes of using that information for commercial gain later. We are not being asked to determine whether Dot Com's Web site alone constitutes the purposeful availment of doing business in Pennsylvania. This is a "doing business over the Internet" case in the line of *Compuserve, supra.* We are being asked to determine whether Dot Com's conducting of electronic commerce with Pennsylvania residents constitutes the purposeful availment of doing business in Pennsylvania. We conclude that it does. Dot Com has contracted with approximately 3,000 individuals and seven Internet access providers in Pennsylvania. The intended object of these transactions has been the downloading of the electronic messages that form the basis of this suit in Pennsylvania.

. . .

Dot Com . . . contends that its contacts with Pennsylvania residents are "fortuitous" within the meaning of *World Wide Volkswagen,* 444 U.S. 286, 62 L. Ed. 2d 490, 100 S. Ct. 559 (1980). Defendant argues that it has not 'actively' solicited business in Pennsylvania and that any business it conducts with Pennsylvania residents has resulted from contacts that were initiated by Pennsylvanians who visited the Defendant's Web site. The fact that Dot Com's services have been consumed in Pennsylvania is not "fortuitous" within the meaning of *World Wide Volkswagen.* . . . Dot Com's contacts with Pennsylvania would be fortuitous within the meaning of *World Wide Volkswagen* if it had no Pennsylvania subscribers and an

If a Web site falls on the interactive middle ground, what level of interactivity is required?

Why does the court distinguish between the presence of a Web site alone and the conducting of e-commerce? What happened to the sliding scale?

Ohio subscriber forwarded a copy of a file he obtained from Dot Com to a friend in Pennsylvania or an Ohio subscriber brought his computer along on a trip to Pennsylvania and used it to access Dot Com's service. That is not the situation here. Dot Com repeatedly and consciously chose to process Pennsylvania residents' applications and to assign them passwords. Dot Com knew that the result of these contracts would be the transmission of electronic messages into Pennsylvania. The transmission of these files was entirely within its control. . . . If Dot Com had not wanted to be amenable to jurisdiction in Pennsylvania, the solution would have been simple—it could have chosen not to sell its services to Pennsylvania residents.

Next, Dot Com argues that its forum–related activities are not numerous or significant enough to create a "substantial connection" with Pennsylvania. Defendant points to the fact that only two percent of its subscribers are Pennsylvania residents. However, the Supreme Court has made clear that even a single contact can be sufficient. *McGee*, 355 U.S. at 223. The test has always focused on the "nature and quality" of the contacts with the forum and not the quantity of those contacts. *International Shoe*, 326 U.S. at 320. The Sixth Circuit also rejected a similar argument in *Compuserve* when it wrote that the contacts were "deliberate and repeated even if they yielded little revenue." *Compuserve*, 89 F.3d at 1265.

We also conclude that the cause of action arises out of Dot Com's forum–related conduct in this case. . . .

. . .

Finally, Dot Com argues that the exercise of jurisdiction would be unreasonable in this case. We disagree. There can be no question that Pennsylvania has a strong interest in adjudicating disputes involving the alleged infringement of trademarks owned by resident corporations. We must also give due regard to the Plaintiff's choice to seek relief in Pennsylvania. *Kulko*, 436 U.S. at 92. These concerns outweigh the burden created by forcing the Defendant to defend the suit in Pennsylvania, especially when Dot Com consciously chose to conduct business in Pennsylvania, pursuing profits from the actions that are now in question. The Due Process Clause is not a "territorial shield to interstate obligations that have been voluntarily assumed." *Burger King*, 471 U.S. at 474.

IV. CONCLUSION

We conclude that this Court may appropriately exercise personal jurisdiction over the Defendant and that venue is proper in this judicial district.

NOTES & QUESTIONS

1. As the *Zippo* court indicates, the framework for jurisdictional analysis need not be significantly changed when the Internet is involved. In the United States, the focus remains on the traditional tests of "minimum contacts" for specific jurisdiction and "systematic and continuous" contacts with the forum state for general jurisdiction. The difficulty presented by the Internet is instead in determining how to characterize contacts that occur solely electronically, especially those that occur via the World Wide Web. Although placing material on a Web site does, in one sense, create a presence everywhere that site is accessible, to find jurisdiction on that limited basis would substantially limit the defense of lack of personal jurisdiction by people who in other contexts would successfully raise it. Accordingly, courts have looked to the different degrees to which the Web might be used to establish a connection to remote jurisdictions. Is the puzzle of personal jurisdiction on the Net a doctrinal question—finding the right analogy? Or is it a policy question having to do with what sorts of activities we want to encourage on the Net?

2. The "sliding scale" analysis employed in *Zippo* has subsequently been adopted by many U.S. courts that have considered the issue. See, *e.g.*, *ALS Scan, Inc. v. Digital Service Consultants, Inc.*, 293 F.3d 707 (4th Cir. 2002); *Mink v. AAAA Dev. LLC*, 190 F.3d 333 (5th Cir. 1999); *Cybersell, Inc. v. Cybersell, Inc.*, 130 F.3d 414 (9th Cir. 1997); *Soma Medical International v. Standard Chartered Bank*, 196 F.3d 1292 (10th Cir. 1999). However, *Zippo* has been criticized by some courts and commentators. Consider the following discussion in *Hy Cite Corp. v. Badbusinessbureau.com, L.L.C.*, 297 F. Supp. 2d 1154, 1160–61 (W.D. Wis. 2004):

> The Court of Appeals for the Seventh Circuit has not yet decided a personal jurisdiction case in the Internet context, though several district courts in this circuit have followed *Zippo*. . . . I am reluctant to fall in line with these courts for two reasons. First, it is not clear why a Web site's level of interactivity should be determinative on the issue of personal jurisdiction. As even courts adopting the *Zippo* test have recognized, a court cannot determine whether personal jurisdiction is appropriate simply by deciding whether a Web site is "passive" or "interactive" (assuming that websites can be readily classified into one category or the other). Even a "passive" Web site may support a finding of jurisdiction if the defendant used its Web site intentionally to harm the plaintiff in the forum state. See *Panavision International, LP v. Toeppen*, 141 F.3d 1316, 1322 (9th Cir. 1998).
>
> *Panavision v. Toeppen* was cited by *Zippo* itself, above. Dennis Toeppen established a Web site at panavision.com that displayed aerial views of Pana, Illinois. Panavision brought a trademark infringement and dilution action against the defendant and the district court upheld personal jurisdiction. Similarly, an "interactive" or commercial Web site may not be sufficient to support jurisdiction if it is not aimed at residents in the forum state. See *GTE New Media Services, Inc. v. Bellsouth Corp.*, 339 U.S. App. D.C. 332, 199 F.3d 1343, 1349–50 (D.C. Cir. 2000). Moreover, regardless of how interactive a Web site is, it cannot form the basis for personal juris-

diction unless a nexus exists between the Web site and the cause of action or unless the contacts through the Web site are so substantial that they may be considered "systematic and continuous" for the purpose of general jurisdiction. Thus, a rigid adherence to the *Zippo* test is likely to lead to erroneous results.

Second, in *Zippo*, the court did not explain under what authority it was adopting a specialized test for the Internet or even why such a test was necessary. The Supreme Court has never held that courts should apply different standards for personal jurisdiction depending on the type of contact involved. To the contrary, the Court "long ago rejected the notion that personal jurisdiction might turn on 'mechanical' tests." *Burger King Corp. v. Rudzewicz*, 471 U.S. 462, 478, 85 L. Ed. 2d 528, 105 S. Ct. 2174 (1985) (quoting *International Shoe*, 326 U.S. at 319). The purpose of the "minimum contacts" test set forth in *International Shoe* was to create a standard flexible enough that specialized tests were not needed. As one judge in this circuit has observed in the context of writing about technology, specialized tests are often "doomed to be shallow and to miss unifying principles." Frank H. Easterbrook, *Cyberspace and the Law of the Horse*, U. Chi. Legal F. 207, 207 (1996). "The best way to learn the law applicable to specialized endeavors is to study general rules." *Id.* Other courts have rejected *Zippo* while noting that traditional principles of due process are sufficient to decide personal jurisdiction questions in the Internet context. See, *e.g.*, *Winfield Collection, Ltd. v. McCauley*, 105 F. Supp. 2d 746, 750 (E.D. Mich. 2000) ("The need for a special Internet–focused test for 'minimum contacts' has yet to be established. It seems to this court that the ultimate question can still as readily be answered by determining whether the defendant did, or did not, have sufficient 'minimum contacts' in the forum state.").

3. Is *Zippo*'s sliding scale helpful for Internet–based cases that have nothing to do with domain names and Web sites? Does it answer where a claim for, say, harassment during an AOL instant

messenger interchange should take place? A claim against AOL for allowing its service to be used for such harassment?

4. Is *Zippo*'s sliding scale helpful for assessing noncommercial Web site activities? Consider the facts of *Zidon v. Pickrell*, 344 F.Supp. 2d 624, (D.N.D. 2004):

> The plaintiff, Patrick Zidon, is a North Dakota resident. The defendant, Linda Pickrell, is a resident of Colorado. Zidon and Pickrell cultivated a romantic relationship after meeting online in September 2000. Zidon ended the relationship in March 2004. Zidon, in a complaint filed on September 21, 2004, alleged that Pickrell created a Web site entitled "Monster of Love: Surviving Love/Sex Addicts and Spiritual Predators" at the domain name www.patrickzidon.com following their breakup, where she posted allegedly defamatory statements. In addition, Zidon alleges Pickrell e-mailed a hyperlink to the Web site to persons in the Bismarck, North Dakota, area as well as the public at large. *Id.* at 626.

Zidon sued for defamation and intentional infliction of emotional distress. Pickrell argued that, based on her limited contacts, she should not be subject to personal jurisdiction in North Dakota. The district court disagreed and found personal jurisdiction over Pickrell to be proper, although the *Zippo* sliding scale was not dispositive. Even though an e-mail link, information about Zidon, and a bulletin board made the Web site "interactive" on *Zippo*'s sliding scale, the court found that such contacts were insufficient to establish personal jurisdiction. Instead, the court relied on the "effects test," an alternative basis for personal jurisdiction when a defendant has directed activity at the forum and caused harm in the forum. *Id.* at 627–33.

II.B. Conflict of Laws and the Convoy Problem

Once a tribunal has effectively asserted jurisdiction over the relevent parties, it must determine what body of substantive law to apply to resolve the controversy. When a would–be defendant is challenging a sovereign's jurisdiction, it is often less the inconvenience or seeming unfairness of having to physically travel long distances to mount a defense, but rather an attempt to avoid falling under the sway of that sovereign's substantive laws.

In the United States, the meta–doctrine that determines which substantive law should be applied is known as "conflict of laws." Internationally, it is thought of as a branch of "private international law."

This is a notoriously unstable, shifting field of doctrine, characterized by warring principles and tests such as the "the most significant relationship" test, the "center of gravity" approach, and the "interest" approach.

The unsettled nature of choice of law in the Internet context, particularly in international disputes, seems to remain because there have, in fact, been few cases brought—or at least brought to reportable conclusion—over alleged damage from faraway networked parties. It is possible that, as a practical matter, the likely defendants are thought by plaintiffs to be judgment–proof, or difficult—as a matter of personal jurisdiction—to effectively bring before the plaintiff's local tribunal.

Be Careful What You Ask For: Reconciling a Global Internet and Local Law (I)
Jonathan Zittrain
Who Rules the Net?, Cato Institute, 2003

> At the state level within the United States, the "dormant commerce clause" of the Constitution is said to proscribe state laws whose effects reach beyond state borders, even if the target of regulation is legitimate within the state. It was by way of this reasoning that a district court struck down a New York law asking Web site operators to ensure that indecent content could not be viewed by minors. (*American Library Association v. Pataki*, 969 F.Supp. 160 (S.D.N.Y. 1997)). The court's view

was that every Web site operator in the country would be affected by such requirements since there was no easy way to know
when a New York minor might stumble onto a given site and
thereby bring its operator under the sway of New York's law.
(969 F. Supp. 160 at 167) States are thus compelled to limit
their lawmaking when an intervention affects parties outside
the state who are otherwise operating under other ground
rules, even as the Federal government is not held to a comparable standard *vis-à-vis* the international community. This
may be doctrinally inconsistent, but it's perfectly understand-
able in the obvious absence of a unifying global legal structure.

AMERICAN LIBRARY ASSOCIATION V. PATAKI
969 F. Supp. 160 (S.D.N.Y. 1997)

[Suit was brought by a group "of individuals and organizations
who use the Internet to communicate, disseminate, display,
and access a broad range of communications," to challenge
a New York State statute that made it illegal to use a computer to communicate to minors any material that was defined by
statute to be "harmful to minors." The statute was modeled
on the federal Communications Decency Act of 1996 and was
also challenged on First Amendment grounds, but the District
Court here granted a preliminary injunction barring enforcement of the statute on the basis of the Commerce Clause of
the U.S. Constitution.]

. . .

II. Federalism and the Internet: The Commerce Clause

The borderless world of the Internet raises profound questions
concerning the relationship among the several states and the
relationship of the federal government to each state, questions that go to the heart of "our federalism." [ ] The Act at

issue in the present case is only one of many efforts by state legislators to control the chaotic environment of the Internet. For example, the Georgia legislature has enacted a recent law prohibiting Internet users from "falsely identifying" themselves online. Ga. Stat. 16-9-9.1. Similar legislation is pending in California. California Senate Bill SB-1533 (1996). [ ] Texas and Florida have concluded that law firm Web pages (apparently including those of out-of-state firms) are subject to the rules of professional conduct applicable to attorney advertising. [ ] Further, states have adopted widely varying approaches in the application of general laws to communications taking place over the Internet. Minnesota has aggressively pursued out-of-state advertisers and service providers who reach Minnesotans via the Internet; Illinois has also been assertive in using existing laws to reach out-of-state actors whose connection to Illinois occurs only by virtue of an Internet communication. [ ] Florida has taken the opposite route, declining to venture into online law enforcement until various legal issues (including, perhaps, the one discussed in the present opinion) have been determined. [ ]

The unique nature of the Internet highlights the likelihood that a single actor might be subject to haphazard, uncoordinated, and even outright inconsistent regulation by states that the actor never intended to reach and possibly was unaware were being accessed. Typically, states' jurisdictional limits are related to geography; geography, however, is a virtually meaningless construct on the Internet. The menace of inconsistent state regulation invites analysis under the Commerce Clause of the Constitution, because that clause represented the framers' reaction to overreaching by the individual states that might jeopardize the growth of the nation—and in particular, the national infrastructure of communications and trade—as a whole. [ ]

The Commerce Clause is more than an affirmative grant of power to Congress. As long ago as 1824, Justice Johnson in his concurring opinion in *Gibbons v. Ogden*, 9 Wheat. 1,

231–32, 239 (1824), recognized that the Commerce Clause has a negative sweep as well. In what commentators have come to term its negative or "dormant" aspect, the Commerce Clause restricts the individual states' interference with the flow of interstate commerce in two ways. The Clause prohibits discrimination aimed directly at interstate commerce, see, *e.g.*, *Philadelphia v. New Jersey*, 437 U.S. 617 (1978), and bars state regulations that, although facially nondiscriminatory, unduly burden interstate commerce, see *e.g.*, *Kassel v. Consolidated Freightways Corp.*, 450 U.S. 662 (1981). Moreover, courts have long held that state regulation of those aspects of commerce that by their unique nature demand cohesive national treatment is offensive to the Commerce Clause. See *e.g.*, *Wabash St. L. & P. Rv. Co. v. Illinois*, 118 U.S. 557 (1887) (holding railroad rates exempt from state regulation).

Is more coordination needed on a national, not state or local, level to regulate conduct potentially harmful to minors?

Thus . . . the New York Act is concerned with interstate commerce and contravenes the Commerce Clause for three reasons. First, the Act represents an unconstitutional projection of New York law into conduct that occurs wholly outside New York. Second, the Act is invalid because although protecting children from indecent material is a legitimate and indisputably worthy subject of state legislation, the burdens on interstate commerce resulting from the Act clearly exceed any local benefit derived from it. Finally, the Internet is one of those areas of commerce that must be marked off as a national preserve to protect users from inconsistent legislation that, taken to its most extreme, could paralyze development of the Internet altogether. Thus, the Commerce Clause ordains that only Congress can legislate in this area, subject, of course, to whatever limitations other provisions of the Constitution (such as the First Amendment) may require.

A. The Act Concerns Interstate Commerce

At oral argument, the defendants advanced the theory that the

Act is aimed solely at intrastate conduct. This argument is unsupportable in light of the text of the statute itself, its legislative history, and the reality of Internet communications . . . .

The conclusion that the Act must apply to interstate as well as intrastate communications receives perhaps its strongest support from the nature of the Internet itself. The Internet is wholly insensitive to geographic distinctions. In almost every case, users of the Internet neither know nor care about the physical location of the Internet resources they access. Internet protocols were designed to ignore rather than document geographic location; while computers on the network do have "addresses," they are logical addresses on the network rather than geographic addresses in real space. The majority of Internet addresses contain no geographic clues and, even where an Internet address provides such a clue, it may be misleading . . . .

Moreover, no aspect of the Internet can feasibly be closed off to users from another state. An Internet user who posts a Web page cannot prevent New Yorkers or Oklahomans or Iowans from accessing that page and will not even know from what state visitors to that site hail. Nor can a participant in a chat room prevent other participants from a particular state from joining the conversation. Someone who uses a mail exploder is similarly unaware of the precise contours of the mailing list that will ultimately determine the recipients of his or her message, because users can add or remove their names from a mailing list automatically. Thus, a person could choose a list believed not to include any New Yorkers, but an after-added New Yorker would still receive the message. [ ]

. . .

The New York Act, therefore, cannot effectively be limited to purely intrastate communications over the Internet because no such communications exist. No user could reliably restrict her communications only to New York recipients. Moreover, no user could avoid liability under the New York Act simply by directing his or her communications elsewhere, given that

there is no feasible way to preclude New Yorkers from accessing a Web site, receiving a mail exploder message or a newsgroup posting, or participating in a chat room. Similarly, a user
has no way to ensure that an e–mail does not pass through
New York even if the ultimate recipient is not located there, or
that a message never leaves New York even if both sender and
recipient are located there.

. . .

The Act is therefore necessarily concerned with interstate
communications. . . . The next question that requires an answer
as a threshold matter is whether the types of communication
involved constitute "commerce" within the meaning of the
Clause.

. . .

The courts have long recognized that railroads, trucks, and
highways are themselves "instruments of commerce,"
because they serve as conduits for the transport of products
and services. See *Kassel v. Consolidated Freightways Corp.*,
450 U.S. 662 (1981); *Southern Pacific Co. v. Arizona*, 325 U.S.
761, 780 (1945). The Internet is more than a means of communication; it also serves as a conduit for transporting digi-
tized goods, including software, data, music, graphics, and
videos which can be downloaded from the provider's site to
the Internet user's computer. For example, plaintiff BiblioBytes
and members of plaintiff IDSA both sell and deliver their products over the Internet.

The inescapable conclusion is that the Internet represents
an instrument of interstate commerce, albeit an innovative
one; the novelty of the technology should not obscure the fact
that regulation of the Internet impels traditional Commerce
Clause considerations. The New York Act is therefore closely
concerned with interstate commerce, and scrutiny of the Act
under the Commerce Clause is entirely appropriate. As discussed in the following sections, the Act cannot survive such

scrutiny, because it places an undue burden on interstate traffic, whether that traffic be in goods, services, or ideas.

B. New York Has Overreached by Enacting a Law That Seeks To Regulate Conduct Occurring Outside its Borders

. . .

In the present case, a number of witnesses testified to the chill that they felt as a result of the enactment of the New York statute; these witnesses refrained from engaging in particular types of interstate commerce. In particular, I note the testimony of Rudolf Kinsky, an artist with a virtual studio on Art on the Net's Web site. Mr. Kinsky testified that he removed several images from his virtual studio because he feared prosecution under the New York Act. (4/7/97 Tr., at 231–35). As described above, no Web site–holder is able to close his site to New Yorkers. Thus, even if Mr. Kinsky were located in California and wanted to display his work to a prospective purchaser in Oregon, he could not employ his virtual studio to do so without risking prosecution under the New York law.

. . .

The nature of the Internet makes it impossible to restrict the effects of the New York Act to conduct occurring within New York. An Internet user may not intend that a message be accessible to New Yorkers, but lacks the ability to prevent New Yorkers from visiting a particular Web site or viewing a particular newsgroup posting or receiving a particular mail exploder. Thus, conduct that may be legal in the state in which the user acts can subject the user to prosecution in New York and thus subordinate the user's home state's policy—perhaps favoring freedom of expression over a more protective stance—to New York's local concerns. See *Bigelow v. Virginia*, 421 U.S. 309, 824 (1975) ("A State does not acquire power or supervision over the internal affairs of another State merely because the welfare and health of its own citizens may be affected when they travel to that State."). New York has deliberately imposed its legislation on the Internet and, by doing so, projected its law into other states whose citizens use the Net. See *Southern Pacific Co. v. Arizona ex ref. Sullivan*, 325 U.S. 761, 774 (1945) ("If one state may regulate train lengths, so may all others, and they need not prescribe the same maximum limitation. The practical effect of [a law limiting train lengths] is to control train operations beyond the boundaries of the state exacting it because of the necessity of breaking up and reassembling long trains at the nearest terminal points before entering and after leaving the regulating state."). This encroachment upon the authority which the Constitution specifically confers upon the federal government and upon the sovereignty of New York's sister states is *per se* violative of the Commerce Clause.

. . .

D. The Act Unconstitutionally Subjects Interstate Use of the Internet to Inconsistent Regulations

. . .The courts have long recognized that certain types of commerce demand consistent treatment and are therefore susceptible to regulation only on a national level. The Internet represents one of those areas; effective regulation will require national, and more likely global, cooperation. Regulation by any single state can only result in chaos, because at least some states will likely enact laws subjecting Internet users to conflicting obligations. Without the limitations imposed by the Commerce Clause, these inconsistent regulatory schemes could paralyze the development of the Internet altogether.

In numerous cases, the Supreme Court has acknowledged the need for coordination in the regulation of certain areas of commerce. As long ago as 1886, the Supreme Court stated:

Commerce with foreign countries and among the states, strictly considered, consists in intercourse and traffic, including in these terms navigation, and the transportation and transit of persons and property, as well as the purchase, sale, and exchange of commodities. For the regulation of commerce, as thus defined, there can be only one system of rules, applicable alike to the whole country; and the authority which can act for the whole country can alone adopt such a system. Action upon it by separate states is not, therefore, permissible.

Wabash, St. L. & P. Ry. Co. v. Illinois, 118 U.S. 557, 574–75 (1886). . . .

The Internet, like the rail and highway traffic. . .requires a cohesive national scheme of regulation so that users are reasonably able to determine their obligations. Regulation on a local level, by contrast, will leave users lost in a welter of inconsistent laws, imposed by different states with different priorities. New York is not the only state to enact a law purporting to regulate the content of communications on the Internet. Already Oklahoma and Georgia have enacted laws designed to protect minors from indecent communications over the Internet; as might be expected, the states have selected different methods to accomplish their aims. Georgia has made it a crime to communicate anonymously over the Internet, while Oklahoma, like New York, has prohibited the online transmission of material deemed harmful to minors. See GA. CODE ANN. § 16–19–93.1 (1996); OKLA. STAT. tit. 21, § 1040.76 (1996).

Moreover, the regulation of communications that may be "harmful to minors" taking place over the Internet poses particular difficulties. New York has defined "harmful to minors" as including:

[T]hat quality of any description or representation, in whatever form, of nudity, sexual conduct, sexual excitement, or sado–masochistic abuse, when it:

(a) Considered as a whole, appeals to the prurient interest in sex of minors; and

(b) Is patently offensive to prevailing standards in the adult community as a whole with respect to what is suitable material for minors; and

(c) Considered as a whole, lacks serious literary, artistic, political and scientific value for minors.

N.Y. Penal Law § 235.20(6). Courts have long recognized, however, that there is no single "prevailing community standard" in the United States. Thus, even were all 50 states to enact laws that were verbatim copies of the New York Act, Internet users would still be subject to discordant responsibilities. To use an example cited by the court in *ACLU v. Reno*, the Broadway play *Angels in America*, which concerns homosexuality and AIDS and features graphic language, was immensely popular in New York and in fact earned two Tony awards and a Pulitzer prize. *ACLU*, 929 F. Supp. at 852–53. In Charlotte, North Carolina, however, a production of the drama caused such a public outcry that the Mecklenberg County Commission voted to withhold all public funding from arts organizations whose works "expose the public to perverted forms of sexuality." [ ] The Supreme Court has always recognized that "our nation is simply too big and too diverse for this Court to reasonably expect that such standards [of what is patently offensive] could be articulated for all 50 states in a single formulation." *Miller*, 413 U.S. at 30.

[A]n Internet user cannot foreclose access to her work from certain states or send differing versions of her communication to different jurisdictions. In this sense, the Internet user is in a worse position than the truck driver or train engineer who can steer around Illinois or Arizona, or change the mudguard or train configuration at the state line; the Internet user has no ability to bypass any particular state. The user must thus comply with the regulation imposed by the state with the most stringent standard or forego Internet communication of the message that might or might not subject her to prosecution. For example, a teacher might invite discussion of *Angels In America* from a Usenet newsgroup dedicated to the literary interests of high school students. Quotations from the play might not subject her to prosecution in New York [ ]—but could qualify as "harmful to minors" according to the community standards prevailing in Oklahoma. The teacher cannot tailor her message on a community specific basis and thus must take her chances or avoid the discussion altogether.

If this is indeed a "slowest ship in the convoy" problem, is the only alternative to allowing the slowest ship to set the pace nationwide one that allows the "fastest ship" to set the pace for everyone?

Further development of the Internet requires that users be able to predict the results of their Internet use with some degree of assurance. Haphazard and uncoordinated state regulation can only frustrate the growth of cyberspace. The need for uniformity in this unique sphere of commerce requires that New York's law be stricken as a violation of the Commerce Clause.

. . .

CONCLUSION

The protection of children from pedophilia is an entirely valid and laudable goal of state legislation. The New York Act's attempts to effectuate that goal, however, fall afoul of the Commerce Clause for three reasons. First, the practical impact of the New York Act results in the extraterritorial application of New York law to transactions involving citizens of other states and is therefore per se violative of the Commerce Clause. Second, the benefits derived from the Act are inconsequential in relation to the severe burdens it imposes on interstate commerce. Finally, the unique nature of cyberspace necessitates uniform national treatment and bars the states from enacting inconsistent regulatory schemes. Because plaintiffs have demonstrated that they are likely to succeed on the merits of their claim under the Commerce Clause and that they face irreparable injury in the absence of an injunction, the motion for a preliminary injunction is granted.

Defendants are enjoined from instituting any prosecutions under the Act, until further Order of this Court. . . . .

SO ORDERED.

The High Court of Australia made waves at the end of 2002 when it handed down its opinion in *Dow Jones & Co., Inc. v. Gutnick* 194 ALR 433 (2002). At issue was the question of whether the defendant, a U.S. corporation, could be required to appear and defend itself against defamation claims brought by Mr. Gutnick, an Australian citizen, in an Australian court. Dow Jones argued that despite selling online subscriptions to Australian customers, publication had occurred in New Jersey where the offending documents were first put up on a Web server and that New Jersey law should therefore apply to the action. If New Jersey law were deemed to control the action, jurisdiction in Australia might be considered "clearly inappropriate" and the plaintiff might have had no other option than to seek redress in U.S. courts. This possibility promised the defendants both a more convenient forum and more sympathetic law to govern the case.

Dow Jones's argument was founded on a special doctrine in U.S. defamation law known as the "single publication rule." The rule is set out in § 577A of the *Restatement of Torts*, 2d (1977), "Single and Multiple Publications." It provides in relevant part:

> (2) A single communication heard at the same time by two or more third persons is a single publication.
> (3) Any one edition of a book or newspaper, or any one radio or television broadcast, exhibition of a motion picture or similar aggregate communication is a single publication.
> (4) As to any single publication,
>> (a) only one action for damages can be maintained;
>> (b) all damages suffered in all jurisdictions can be recovered in the one action; and
>> (c) a judgment for or against the plaintiff upon the merits of any action for damages bars any other action for damages between the same parties in all jurisdictions.

As the *Gutnick* court observed, it was not until the advent of widely disseminated mass media of communication in the middle of the twentieth century that choice of law problems were identified in the defamation context:

> [T]hen, by a process of what was understood as logical extension of the single publication rule, the choice of law to be applied came to be understood as largely affected by, perhaps even to be determined by, the proposition that only one action could be brought in respect of the alleged defamation and that the place

of publication was where the person publishing the words had acted. *Gutnick*, 194 ALR at n.32.

The court indicated that it believed that the extension of the single publication rule to the realm of choice of law to be confusing two separate questions: "one about how to prevent multiplicity of suits and vexation of parties, and the other about what law must be applied to determine substantive questions arising in an action in which there are foreign elements." *Id*, at n.35.

BE CAREFUL WHAT YOU ASK FOR: RECONCILING A GLOBAL INTERNET AND LOCAL LAW (II)
Jonathan Zittrain
Who Rules the Net?, Cato Institute, 2003

As a government reflects on the proper limits of its reach against a faraway defendant whose Internet activities are causing local grief, it runs into a dilemma. On the one hand, a plaintiff might claim it unfair that the sovereign would decline to intervene simply because a defendant is wholly absent, since the effects of the defendant's Internet behavior are still felt locally. On the other hand, going on an "effects" test alone suggests that anyone posting information on the Internet is unduly open to nearly any sovereign's jurisdiction, since that information could have an effect around the world. Prof. Geist . . . suggests a middle path, that of "targeting," where something more than effects, but less than physical presence, could trigger jurisdiction. That path tries to peel away many if not all extraneous governments from a scrum that could pile up around a single defendant's objectionable behavior, while preserving the prospect that jurisdictions other than the defendant's home could stake a legitimate claim to intervene. As with many middle paths, the devil lies in the details. But especially in the midst of a sea change in the fundamental global Internet/local law dilemma—one where a more localized Internet is possible thanks to geolocation technologies—such a path seems the best compromise in an inherently difficult situation.

The High Court of Australia's decision in *Gutnick v. Dow Jones* [ ] vindicates this kind of reasoning in a case that blends personal jurisdiction with choice of law. There, an Australian businessman named Joseph Gutnick sued Dow Jones for an unflattering portrait of him published online in *Barron's.* Dow Jones asked the Australian legal system to decline to intervene, arguing that Dow Jones's United States home was the fairest place to hear the dispute. The Australian court was unpersuaded by the "pile on" argument that Gutnick could next sue the company in Zimbabwe, or Great Britain, or China. It pointed out that Gutnick himself lived in Australia, and Dow Jones quite explicitly sold subscriptions to the online *Barron's* to Australians. These facts helped Australia escape the dilemma of justifying almost any country's intervention if it was to justify its own. Without its special if not unique relationship to one party in the case, Australia may well have declined to intervene in the dispute.

Even as the pure issue of "personal jurisdiction" finds a messy lawyer's compromise, when people or companies are far away from a sovereign's physical territory—or anonymous, and therefore of unknown location—the sovereign's quandaries more typically involve reconciling its laws with those of other governments that might similarly find a right to intervene, or bareknuckle enforcement of any decrees it enacts against a faraway party once it has assured itself of its right to intervene.

The Court concluded that since, under Australian law, defamation actions are located at the place where the damage to reputation occurs, and since "it is . . . established that in trying an action for tort in which the parties or the events have some connection with a jurisdiction outside Australia, the choice of law rule to be applied is that matters of substance are governed by the law of the place of commission of the tort," *Dow Jones,* 194 ALR at n.5, Australian law would apply to the dispute and thus that Victoria, Australia, was not a "clearly inappropriate forum" for the action.

Dow Jones's primary argument had focused on the spectre of "a publisher forced to consider every article it published on the World Wide Web against the defamation laws of every country from Afghanistan to Zimbabwe." The Court responded to this fear with the observation that "in all except the most unusual of cases, identifying the person about whom material is to be published will readily identify the defamation law to which that person may resort."

NOTES & QUESTIONS

1. In *Twentieth Century Fox Film Corp. v. ICraveTV,* 2000 WL 255989 (W.D.Pa. Feb. 8, 2000), several large media content providers brought suit in the U.S. District Court for the Western District of Pennsylvania against a Canadian company that was streaming the plaintiffs' copyrighted content over the Internet in violation of U.S. law. The defendant argued that its Web site was intended for Canadian viewers only and not for viewers in the United States or elsewhere, and thus that the alleged improper acts were limited to Canada. The defendant submitted a declaration of Canadian law professor Michael Geist that argued that the defendant's actions were permissible under Canadian copyright law. The court dismissed that argument with the explanation that "[b]ecause plaintiffs seek relief under U.S. law for infringements of the U.S. Copyright Act, there is no need for this Court to address any issue of Canadian law."

2. Courts have departed from the reasoning in *Pataki* to uphold the constitutionality of state spam statutes despite the Commerce Clause. In *Ferguson v. Friendfinders, Inc.,* 115 Cal. Rptr. 2d 258 (Cal. Ct. App. 2002), the court upheld the constitutionality of §

17538.4 of the California Business and Professions Code, an anti–spam law that "regulates individuals and entities that (1) do business in California, (2) utilize equipment located in California, and (3) send [unsolicited commercial e–mail] to California residents." *Id.* at 264. Explicitly rejecting *Pataki's* holding, *Id.* at 265, the court found that the law "does not discriminate against or directly regulate or control interstate commerce; thus it is valid if it serves a legitimate local public interest and if the burden it imposes on interstate commerce is not excessive when viewed in light of its local benefits." *Id.* at 258. See also *State v. Heckel*, 24 P.3d 404 (Wash. 2001).

3. State anti–spam laws may have constitutional deficiencies under the First Amendment. In *American Civil Liberties Union of Georgia v. Miller*, 977 F. Supp. 1228 (N.D.Ga. 1997), the court granted a preliminary injunction against enforcement of a Georgia statute which made it a crime "for any person . . . knowingly to transmit any data through a computer network . . . if such data uses any individual name . . . to falsely identify the person" or "if such data uses any . . . trade name, registered trademark, logo, legal or official seal, or copyrighted symbol . . . which would falsely state or imply that such person . . . has permission or is legally authorized to use [it] for such purpose when such permission or authorization has not been obtained." *Id.* at 1230. The court found that the plaintiffs were likely to succeed on their claims that "the statute imposes content–based restrictions which are not narrowly tailored to achieve the state's purported compelling interest" and that "the statute is overbroad and void for vagueness." *Id.* at 1232.

4. The High Court of Australia in *Gutnick* largely rejected Dow Jones's argument that a *Zippo*–like interactivity rationale should apply to the jurisdictional analysis. "[M]uch weight appears to have been placed by Dow Jones on the contention that a relevant distinction was to be drawn between the apparently passive role played by a person placing material on a Web server from which the would–be reader had actively to seek the material by use of a Web browser and the (comparatively) active role

played by a publisher of a widely circulated newspaper or a widely disseminated radio or television broadcast." *Gutnick,* 194 ALR at n.9. The High Court found the *Zippo*–like reasoning flawed for failing to consider the balance of interests that defamation law seeks to regulate. The High Court ultimately relied on language more akin to the "effects test" used by the court in *Zidon v. Pickrell, supra:* "Activities that have effects beyond the jurisdiction in which they are done may properly be the concern of the legal systems in each place." *Id.* at n.11.

5. To allay any fears that the publisher defendants had about being called into court in any country in the world based on Web publications, the *Gutnick* court pointed out that that "plaintiffs are unlikely to sue for defamation published outside the forum unless a judgment obtained in the action would be of real value to the plaintiff. The value that a judgment would have may be affected by whether it can be enforced in a place where the defendant has assets." This is the jurisdictional factor to which we now turn.

II.C. Enforcement of Judgments

Of course, the judgment of a court is only meaningful to the extent that it can be enforced. A sovereign can enforce the judgments of its courts only insofar as a defendant or his or her assets can be reached by the enforcement mechanisms of the sovereign, the sovereign can get extradition of an absent defendant from some other sovereign, or foreign states will enforce the judgment of the sovereign on its behalf. Within the United States, all three of these enforcement methods are available among states: the first by exercise of police power, the second for enforcement of criminal laws, and the third by requirement of the Full Faith and Credit Clause of the Constitution. Internationally, the problem is more complicated and is governed by doctrines of "international comity." As illustrated by a U.S. district court decision in the *Yahoo! France* case, a court generally will not enforce a foreign judgment it views as contrary to the U.S. Constitution.

II.C.1. Sealand / HavenCo

Motivated by a vision for the autonomy of cyberspace—and by potential profits—HavenCo is a start–up company seeking to deliver for its customers the government–free vision of the Internet described by Barlow. It aims to realize this vision through very practical, direct means: HavenCo has deployed its network on Sealand, an independent sovereignty that consists of an abandoned British island fortress in international waters. As described by the Web site of the Sealand government at http://www.sealand-gov.com/:

> Sealand was founded as a sovereign Principality in 1967 in international waters, six miles off the eastern shores of Britain. The island fortress is conveniently situated from 65 to 100 miles from the coasts of France, Belgium, Holland and Germany. The official language of Sealand is English and the Sealand Dollar has a fixed exchange rate of one U.S. dollar. Passports and stamps have been in circulation since 1969, however, contrary to many misleading websites and news articles, Sealand passports are not for sale, and anyone offering such are selling forgeries. Within a radius of 500 miles of Sealand live more than 200 million people who enjoy some of the highest standards of living in the world. This area also encompasses the financial, industrial and cultural heart of Europe.

> The history of Sealand is a story of a struggle for liberty. Sealand was founded on the principle that any group of people dissatisfied with the oppressive laws and restrictions of existing nation states may declare independence in any place not claimed to be under the jurisdiction of another sovereign entity. The location chosen was Roughs Tower, an island fortress created in World War II by Britain and subsequently abandoned to the jurisdiction of the High Seas. The independence of Sealand was upheld in a 1968 British court decision where the judge held that Roughs Tower stood in international waters and did not fall under the legal jurisdiction of the

United Kingdom. This gave birth to Sealand's national motto of *E Mare Libertas*, or "From the Sea, Freedom."

WELCOME TO SEALAND. NOW BUGGER OFF.
Simson Garfinkel
Wired, July 2000

Hunkered down on a North Sea fortress, a crew of armed cypherpunks, amped-up networking geeks, and libertarian swashbucklers is seceding from the world to pursue a revolutionary idea: an offshore, fat-pipe data haven that answers to nobody.

Ryan Lackey, a 21-year-old MIT dropout and self-taught crypto expert, sees fantastic things for himself in 2005. For starters, he'll be filthy rich. But his future is animated by more than just money—to wit, the exploration of a huge idea he thinks will change the world. Lackey's big concept? That freedom is the next killer app.

Before you get too choked up, you should know that Lackey means giving corporations and frisky individuals the "freedom" to store and move data without answering to anybody, including competitors, regulators, and lawyers. He's part of a crew of adventurers and cypherpunks that's working to transform a 60-year-old gunnery fort in the North Sea—an odd, quasi-independent outpost whose British owner calls it "the Principality of Sealand"—into something that could be possible only in the 21st century: a fat-pipe Internet server farm and global networking hub that combines the spicier elements of a Caribbean tax shelter, Cryptonomicon, and 007.

[In the summer of 2000], with $1 million in seed money provided by a small core of Internet-fattened investors, Lackey and his colleagues [set] up Sealand as the world's first truly offshore, almost-anything-goes electronic data haven—a place that occupies a tantalizing gray zone between what's legal and what's . . . possible. Especially if you exist, as the Sealanders plan to, outside the jurisdiction of the world's nation-states. Simply put: Sealand won't just be offshore. It will be off-government.

The startup is called, fittingly, HavenCo Ltd. Headquartered on a 6,000-square-foot, World War II-era antiaircraft deck that comprises the "land" of Sealand, the facility isn't much to look at and probably never will be. It consists of a rusty steel deck sitting on two hollow, chubby concrete cylinders that rise 60 feet above the churn of the North Sea. Up top there's a drab building and a jury-rigged helicopter landing pad.

Soon, Lackey believes, powerful upgrades will transform Sealand into something amazing. The huge support cylinders will contain millions of dollars' worth of networking gear: computers, servers, transaction processors, data-storage devices—all cooled with banks of roaring air conditioners and powered by triple-redundant generators. HavenCo will provide its clients with nearly a gigabit per second of Internet bandwidth by year's end, at prices far cheaper than those on the overregulated dry land of Europe—whose financial capitals sit a mere 20 milliseconds away from Sealand's electronic nerve center. Three speedy connections to HavenCo affiliate hubs all over the planet—microwave, satellite, and underwater fiber-optic links—will ensure that the data never stops flowing.

HavenCo's onboard staff will come and go on helicopters and speedboats. Four security people will be on hand at all times to maintain order; six computer geeks will run the network operations center. The security personnel, heavily armed and ready to blast anybody who shouldn't be around, will make sure that unauthorized boats and aircraft keep their distance. The geeks will perform maintenance tasks like replacing failed hard disks and installing new equipment. These routine chores will be a little more challenging than usual, given the maritime setting and Sealand's obsession with privacy. Fall over the edge of Sealand's deck, for instance, and you'll probably drown.

Simply entering one of the machine rooms will require putting on scuba gear, because the rooms will be filled with an unbreathable pure nitrogen atmosphere instead of the normal oxygen mix—a measure designed to keep out sneaks, inhibit rust, and reduce the risk of fire.

HavenCo will be "offshore" both physically and in the sense that its clients—who will purchase preconfigured "colocation" computers maintained and secured by HavenCo—will basically be able to tell the rest of the world to shove it. The essence of offshore Internet services, as defined by sort-of-offshore places like Anguilla and Bermuda, is that when you base an operation in such a locale, you can claim to be governed only by the laws that prevail there. So if Internet gambling is legal (or overlooked) in Country A but not in Country B, you set up in A, and use the Web to send your site to B—and to the rest of the world.

Similarly, companies using Sealand to house their data can choose to operate according to the special laws of Sealand, and those laws will be particularly lax—though not quite anarchic. Lackey says the general idea is to allow a little naughtiness, while forbidding criminal activity that could generate international outrage.

Meaning? Basically, that HavenCo wants to give people a safe, secure shelter from lawyers, government snoops, and assorted busybodies without getting tangled in flagrant wrongdoing. So if you run a financial institution that's looking to operate an anonymous and untraceable payment system—HavenCo can help. If you'd like to send old-fashioned, adults-only pornography into a grumpy country like Saudi Arabia—HavenCo can help there, too. But if you want to run a spamming operation, launder drug money, or send kiddie porn anywhere—forget it.

BE CAREFUL WHAT YOU ASK FOR: RECONCILING A GLOBAL INTERNET AND LOCAL LAW (III)
Jonathan Zittrain
Who Rules the Net?, Cato Institute, 2003

... [J]urisdiction based on the movement of bits alone has typically proven too expansive for sovereigns to routinely recognize it. As demonstrated by the use of the *in rem* provisions only as a backstop should the defendant be otherwise unreachable, there are usually other paths to asserting both personal power over a defendant and a subject matter interest in a case. When those paths are lacking, chances are good that the transit of bits will not and should not interest a sovereign—except in cases where a sovereign already has practical enforcement power over a defendant and is satisfied with the slimmest of procedural pretexts to claim the right to intervene. The long-term *storage* of bits in a particular physical location might trigger interest by a government with power over that location, but so long as the storage is not inadvertent or uncontrollable by whatever entity is the source of the data in question, would-be defendants can choose to store data in the most hospitable physical legal environment—while still having it available worldwide through the Internet.

The existence of the so-called Principality of Sealand brings this into perfect relief. A cyberlaw textbook author's dream, Sealand is an abandoned World War II anti-aircraft platform just off the coast of Great Britain. A man named Roy Bates claimed it for his own in the mid-60's, and cites the ambiguous outcome of some U.K. court battles over its ownership—and a failed invasion attempt by German nationals in the 70's—as evidence that it is indeed a sovereign nation.

The most recent use to which Sealand has been put is as the home of a company called HavenCo, which touts itself as providing "the world's most secure managed servers in the world's only true free market environment." [ ] If the storage of data alone were the anchor for the assertion of jurisdiction, data could simply be stored somewhere, such as on Sealand, that would be out of reach of the sovereigns that might have an interest in exercising jurisdiction. Interestingly, Sealand and HavenCo themselves ban the use of their servers to host child pornography—as defined by U.S. law—or to mount hacking or spamming activities. [ ] This could simply reflect Prince Roy's sense of right and wrong, but no doubt also results from the fact that Sealand itself must get its network connectivity somewhere—and could be at risk of losing it should its own Internet service providers reject its activities, or be pressured by nearby governments to do so. Further, the benefits to a would–be defendant of safeguarding data there for jurisdictionally evasive purposes are limited by the defendant's location. Unless a person is willing to move to Sealand, he or she would still be within another sovereign's physical and therefore legal reach and would thus risk being personally penalized should undesired activities taking place on Sealand under the defendant's direction not cease, or sought–after data secured there not be produced.

This is why, while intriguing from an academic standpoint, the existence of Sealand doesn't much change the nature of the jurisdiction and governance debates. It's less about where the bits themselves are, and more about where the people authoring them—and allegedly causing harm by them—are.

NOTES & QUESTIONS

1. How much of a threat is Sealand to other governments that wish to assert control over behavior on the Internet?

2. If you were responsible for safeguarding digital corporate documents as much as possible against intrusion and compromise, including legal process, and resolved to do so as much as possible within the limit of relevant law, would Sealand's services be of use?

3. If you were the U.S. Attorney General and believed there was material on Sealand servers that was illegal to transmit to

Americans (and illegal for them to solicit), what would you do? How effectively could you act against it?

4. It is important to stress that Sealand maintains its own laws with respect to use of the Internet. Thus, to the extent that HavenCo represents the most radical implementation of a "government–free" Internet, it is, itself, subject to regulation by the Sealand government. Is HavenCo ultimately regulated by whoever provides Internet connectivity to Sealand, or whoever can regulate whoever is providing Internet connectivity to Sealand?

5. The true measure of protection afforded to HavenCo customers remains unclear. In spite of the fact that HavenCo is situated in international waters, a U.S. company, for example, would still have to comply with a U.S. court's order requiring production of data stored on Sealand or face contempt charges. Could HavenCo enable a company to avoid subjecting itself to the personal jurisdiction of any country? To what extent are HavenCo's customers likely to escape enforcement of judgments against them simply by virtue of being HavenCo customers?

II.C.2. Enforcement of Judgments: Yahoo! France Part I

YAHOO! v. LA LIGUE CONTRE LE RACISME ET L'ANTISEMITISME AND L'UNION DES ETUDIANTS JUIFS DE FRANCE

169 F. Supp. 2d 1181 (N.D.Cal. 2001)

FOGEL, Jeremy.

I. PROCEDURAL HISTORY

Defendants *La Ligue Contre le Racisme et l'Antisemitisme* ("LICRA") and *L'Union des Etudiants Juifs de France*, citizens of France, are nonprofit organizations dedicated to eliminating anti–Semitism. Plaintiff Yahoo!, Inc. ("Yahoo!") is a corporation organized under the laws of Delaware with its principal place of business in Santa Clara, California. Yahoo! is an Internet service provider that operates various Internet Web sites and services that any computer user can access at . . . http://www.yahoo.com. Yahoo! services ending in the suffix, ".com," without an associated country code as a prefix or extension (collectively, "Yahoo!'s U.S. Services") use the English language and target users who are residents of, utilize servers based in, and operate under the laws of the United States. Yahoo! subsidiary corporations operate regional Yahoo! sites and services in twenty other nations, including, for example, Yahoo! France, Yahoo! India, and Yahoo! Spain. Each of these regional Web sites contains the host nation's unique two–letter code as either a prefix or a suffix in its URL (e.g., Yahoo! France is found at http://www.yahoo.fr.) . . . . Yahoo!'s regional sites use the local region's primary language, target the local citizenry, and operate under local laws.

Yahoo! provides a variety of means by which people from all over the world can communicate and interact with one another over the Internet . . . [including] an Internet search engine, e–mail, an automated auction site, personal Web page hostings, shopping services, chat rooms . . . . Any computer user with Internet access is able to post materials on many of these Yahoo! Sites . . . . As relevant here, Yahoo!'s auction site allows anyone to post an item for sale and solicit bids from any computer user from around the globe . . . . Yahoo! is never a party to a transaction, and the buyer and seller are responsible for arranging privately for payment and shipment of goods. Yahoo! monitors the transaction through limited regulation by prohibiting particular items from being sold (such as stolen goods, body parts, prescription and illegal drugs, weapons, and goods violating U.S. copyright laws or the Iranian and Cuban embargos) . . . . Yahoo! informs auction sellers that they must comply with Yahoo!'s policies and may not offer items to buyers in jurisdictions in which the sale of such item violates the jurisdiction's applicable laws. Yahoo! does not actively regulate the content of each posting, and individuals are able to post, and have in fact posted, highly offensive matter, including Nazi–related propaganda and Third Reich memorabilia, on Yahoo!'s auction sites.

On or about April 5, 2000, LICRA sent a "cease and desist" letter to Yahoo!'s Santa Clara headquarters [in California] informing Yahoo! that the sale of Nazi and Third Reich related goods . . . . violates French law. LICRA threatened to take legal action unless Yahoo! took steps to prevent such sales. . . . Defendants subsequently utilized the United States Marshal's Office to serve Yahoo! with process in California and filed a civil complaint against Yahoo! in. . . (the "French Court").

On May 20, 2000, the French Court entered an order requiring Yahoo! to (1) eliminate French citizens' access to any material on the Yahoo.com auction site that offers for sale any Nazi objects, relics, insignia, emblems, and flags; (2) eliminate French citizens' access to Web pages on Yahoo.com displaying text, extracts, or quotations from *Mein Kampf* and *Protocol of the Elders of Zion;* (3) post a warning to French citizens on Yahoo.fr that any search through Yahoo.com may lead to sites containing material prohibited . . . [under French law]; (4) remove from all browser directories accessible in the French Republic index headings entitled "negationists" and from all hypertext links the equation of "negationists" under the heading "Holocaust." The order subjects Yahoo! to a penalty of 100,000 Euros for each day that it fails to comply with the order. The order concludes:

> We order the Company YAHOO! Inc. to take all necessary measures to dissuade and render impossible any access via Yahoo.com to the Nazi artifact auction service and to any other site or service that may be construed as constituting an apology for Nazism or a contesting of Nazi crimes.
>
>   . . .

Yahoo! . . . [claimed] that although it easily could post the required warning on Yahoo.fr, compliance with the order's requirements with respect to Yahoo.com was technologically impossible. The French Court . . . "reaffirmed" . . . [and] ordered Yahoo! to comply . . . within three (3) months or face a penalty of 100,000 Francs (approximately U.S. $13,300) for each day of noncompliance. The French Court also provided that penalties assessed against Yahoo! Inc. may not be collected from Yahoo! France. Defendants again utilized the United States Marshal's Office to serve Yahoo! in California with the French Order.

. . .

Yahoo! claims that because it lacks the technology to block French citizens from accessing the Yahoo.com auction site to view materials which violate the French Order or from accessing other Nazi–based content of websites on Yahoo.com, it cannot comply with the French order without banning Nazi–related material from Yahoo.com altogether. Yahoo! contends that such a ban would infringe impermissibly upon its rights under the First Amendment to the United States Constitution. Accordingly, Yahoo! filed a complaint in this Court seeking a declaratory judgment that the French Court's orders are neither cognizable nor enforceable under the laws of the United States.

Defendants immediately moved to dismiss on the basis that this Court lacks personal jurisdiction over them. That motion was denied. Defendants' request that the Court certify its jurisdictional determination for interlocutory appeal was denied without prejudice pending the outcome of Yahoo!'s motion for summary judgment.

II. OVERVIEW

As this Court and others have observed, the instant case presents novel and important issues arising from the global reach of the Internet. Indeed, the specific facts of this case implicate issues of policy, politics, and culture that are beyond the purview of one nation's judiciary. Thus it is critical that the Court define at the outset what is and is not at stake in the present proceeding.

This case is not about the moral acceptability of promoting the symbols or propaganda of Nazism. Most would agree that such acts are profoundly offensive.

. . .

Nor is this case about the right of France or any other nation to determine its own law and social policies. A basic function of a sovereign state is to determine by law what forms of speech and conduct are acceptable within its borders. In this instance, as a nation whose citizens suffered the effects of Nazism in ways that are incomprehensible to most Americans, France clearly has the right to enact and enforce laws such as those relied upon by the French Court here.

What is at issue here is whether it is consistent with the Constitution and laws of the United States for another nation to regulate speech by a United States resident within the United States on the basis that such speech can be accessed by Internet users in that nation. In a world in which ideas and information transcend borders and the Internet in particular renders the physical distance between speaker and audience virtually meaningless, the implications of this question go far beyond the facts of this case. The modern world is home to widely varied cultures with radically divergent value systems. There is little doubt that Internet users in the United States routinely engage in speech that violates, for example, China's laws against religious expression, the laws of various nations against advocacy of gender equality or homosexuality, or even the United Kingdom's restrictions on freedom of the press. If the government or another party in one of these sovereign nations were to seek enforcement of such laws against Yahoo! or another U.S.–based Internet service provider, what principles should guide the court's analysis?

The Court has stated that it must and will decide this case in accordance with the Constitution and laws of the United States. It recognizes that in so doing, it necessarily adopts certain value judgments embedded in those enactments, including the fundamental judgment expressed in the First Amendment that it is preferable to permit the non-violent expression of offensive viewpoints rather than to impose viewpoint-based governmental regulation upon speech. The government and people of France have made a different judgment based upon their own experience. In undertaking its inquiry as to the proper application of the laws of the United States, the Court intends no disrespect for that judgment or for the experience that has informed it.

. . .

V. CONCLUSION

Yahoo! seeks a declaration from this Court that the First Amendment precludes enforcement within the United States of a French order intended to regulate the content of its speech over the Internet. Yahoo! has shown that the French order is valid under the laws of France, that it may be enforced with retroactive penalties, and that the ongoing possibility of its enforcement in the United States chills Yahoo!'s First Amendment rights. Yahoo! also has shown that an actual controversy exists and that the threat to its constitutional rights is real and immediate. Defendants have failed to show the existence of a genuine issue of material fact or to identify any such issue the existence of which could be shown through further discovery. Accordingly, the motion for summary judgment will be granted.

Why do you think the defendants' motion was dismissed? How were the requirements for jurisdiction under U.S. law satisfied in their case?

. . .

IT IS SO ORDERED.

NOTES & QUESTIONS

1. If the defendants appealed the ruling on their motion to dismiss based on lack of personal jurisdiction, would they be likely to succeed? Where would Yahoo! stand if the U.S. courts declined to exercise jurisdiction over the French parties? What would the French parties gain if they were able to avoid being subject to the jurisdiction of a court in the United States?

2. In its November 22, 2000, order the French Court specified that the fine it imposed was to be paid by Yahoo!, not by Yahoo! France. Is there any way for the French parties to collect the damages from Yahoo! without subjecting themselves to jurisdiction in the United States by filing suit in the U.S. for enforcement of the French court's judgment?

3. LICRA and *L'Union des Etudiants Juifs de France* ("UEJF") subsequently appealed the district court's decision. The Ninth Circuit reversed, rejecting the District Court contention that it exercised personal jurisdiction over LICRA and UEJF since LICRA and UEJF have yet to seek enforcement through a U.S. court: "France is within its rights as a sovereign nation to enact hate speech laws against the distribution of Nazi propaganda in response to its terrible experience with Nazi forces during World War II. Similarly, LICRA and UEJF are within their rights to bring suit in France against Yahoo! for violation of French speech law. The only adverse consequence experienced by Yahoo! as a result of these acts is that Yahoo! must wait for LICRA and UEJF to come to the United States to enforce the French judgment before it is able to raise its First Amendment claim. However, it was not wrong for the French organizations to place Yahoo! in this position." *Yahoo! Inc. v. La Ligue Contre le Racisme et l'Antisemitisme* 379 F.3d 1120, 1126 (9th Cir. 2004).

4. On March 25, 2005, an en banc panel of the Ninth Circuit heard arguments regarding the appeal of the earlier three–judge Ninth Circuit panel. *Yahoo v. La Ligue Contre le Racisme et l'Antisemitisme*, 399 F. 3d 1010 (2005).

5. In *ICrave*, the U.S. court says that ICrave's compliance with Canadian law is irrelevant because at issue is a violation of U.S. copyright law. In *Yahoo!*, the U.S. court says that the First Amendment protects Yahoo! from enforcement of French laws. Are these opinions able to be reconciled with one another in a principled manner? Or is the U.S., like many other sovereigns would, simply trying to give the maximum protection to its own citizens?

III. BORDERS AND ZONING IN CYBERSPACE

The fundamental problem of Internet jurisdiction is reconciling the Internet's global character with any given local sovereign's desire to regulate. Two broad ways to resolve this dilemma point in opposite directions. First, one might ask sovereigns to abstain from regulation, perhaps because one views cyberspace as its own place capable of self–regulation (or in need of no regulation at all). Second, one might try to change the perceived character of the Internet from that of a global medium to that of a more local one. If one could sort out where any given Internet user was located, that user's activities might be subject to his or her local sovereign's laws without unduly burdening other faraway Internet users. Part A of this section explores the first approach, and Part B the second.

III.A. Global Internet, Global Law: Cyberspace as Its Own Jurisdiction

LAW AND BORDERS: THE RISE OF LAW IN CYBERSPACE
David R. Johnson and David G. Post
48 Stan. L. Rev. 1367 (1996)

> Global electronic communications have created new spaces in which distinct rule sets will evolve. We can reconcile the new law created in this space with current territorially–based legal systems by treating it as a distinct doctrine, applicable to a clearly demarcated sphere, created primarily by legitimate, self–regulatory processes, and entitled to appropriate defer-

ence—but also subject to limitations when it oversteps its appropriate sphere.

The law of any given place must take into account the special characteristics of the space it regulates and the types of persons, places, and things found there. Just as a country's jurisprudence reflects its unique historical experience and culture, the law of Cyberspace will reflect its special character, which differs markedly from anything found in the physical world. For example, the law of the Net must deal with persons who "exist" in Cyberspace only in the form of an e-mail address and whose purported identity may or may not accurately correspond to physical characteristics in the real world. In fact, an e-mail address might not even belong to a single person. Accordingly, if Cyberspace law is to recognize the nature of its "subjects," it cannot rest on the same doctrines that give geographically based sovereigns jurisdiction over "whole," locatable, physical persons. The law of the Net must be prepared to deal with persons who manifest themselves only by means of a particular ID, user account, or domain name.

Who would Johnson & Post say are the "subjects" of cyberlaw?

Moreover, if rights and duties attach to an account itself, rather than an underlying real world person, traditional concepts such as "equality," "discrimination," or even "rights and duties" may not work as we normally understand them. New angles on these ideas may develop. For example, when AOL users joined the Net in large numbers, other Cyberspace users often ridiculed them based on the ".aol" tag on their e-mail addresses—a form of "domainism" that might be discouraged by new forms of Netiquette. If a doctrine of Cyberspace law accords rights to users, we will need to decide whether those rights adhere only to particular types of online appearances, as distinct from attaching to particular individuals in the real world.

Similarly, the types of "properties" that can become the subject of legal discussion in Cyberspace will differ from real world real estate or tangible objects. For example, in the real world the physical covers of a book delineate the boundaries of a "work" for purposes of copyright law; those limits may disappear entirely when the same materials are part of a large electronic database. Thus, we may have to change the "fair use" doctrine in copyright law that previously depended on calculating what portion of the physical work was copied. Similarly, a Web page's "location" in Cyberspace may take on a value unrelated to the physical place where the disk holding that Web page resides, and efforts to regulate Web pages by attempting to control physical objects may only cause the relevant bits to move from one place to another. On the other hand, the boundaries set by "URLs" (Uniform Resource Locators, the location of a document on the World Wide Web) may need special protection against confiscation or confusingly similar addresses. And, because these online "places" may contain offensive material, we may need rules requiring (or allowing) groups to post certain signs or markings at these places' outer borders.

The boundaries that separate persons and things behave differently in the virtual world but are nonetheless legally significant. Messages posted under one e-mail name will not affect the reputation of another e-mail address, even if the same physical person authors both messages. Materials separated by a password will be accessible to different sets of users, even if those materials physically exist on the very same hard drive. A user's claim to a right to a particular online identity or to redress when that identity's reputation suffers harm, may be valid even if that identity does not correspond exactly to that of any single person in the real world.

How does Johnson and Post's argument relate to Barlow's earlier Creed?

Clear boundaries make law possible, encouraging rapid differentiation between rule sets and defining the subjects of legal discussion. New abilities to travel or exchange information rapidly across old borders may change the legal frame of reference and require fundamental changes in legal institutions. Fundamental activities of lawmaking—accommodating conflicting claims, defining property rights, establishing rules to guide conduct, enforcing those rules, and resolving disputes—remain very much alive within the newly defined, intangible territory of Cyberspace. At the same time, the newly emerging law challenges the core idea of a current law–making authority—the territorial nation state, with substantial but legally restrained powers.

If the rules of Cyberspace thus emerge from consensually based rule sets, and the subjects of such laws remain free to move among many differing online spaces, then considering the actions of Cyberspace's system administrators as the exercise of a power akin to "sovereignty" may be inappropriate. Under a legal framework where the top level imposes physical order on those below it and depends for its continued effectiveness on the inability of its citizens to fight back or leave the territory, the legal and political doctrines we have evolved over the centuries are essential to constrain such power. In that situation, where exit is impossible, costly, or painful, then a right to a voice for the people is essential. But when the "persons" in question are not whole people, when their "property" is intangible and portable, and when all concerned may readily escape a jurisdiction they do not find empowering, the relationship between the "citizen" and the "state" changes radically. Law, defined as a thoughtful group conversation about core values, will persist. But it will not, could not, and should not be the same law as that applicable to physical, geographically–defined territories.

NOTES & QUESTIONS

1. What exactly are Johnson and Post predicting or calling for? Are they viewing "cyberspace" as its own jurisdiction, a set of jurisdictions, or something else entirely? What sort of tribunal, if any, are they envisioning to settle disputes?

2. What accounts for their interest in "exit" as a characteristic of online interaction? How might it be applied in a concrete example on the Net?

3. It is interesting to note that Johnson and Post are not talking about wanting a *single* separate rule set for cyberspace, but a separate set of competing rule sets. The choice of law approach suggested by this notion would allow different online spaces to apply their own rule sets without consideration of what other rule sets might arguably apply. The acceptability of this approach appears to rest on the possibility of exit; it would avoid, more than possible in the "real world," the imposition of rules on people who have not consented to be ruled by them.

4. Could Johnson and Post's proposal potentially exacerbate jurisdictional issues by increasing intra–Internet disputes (*e.g.*, ISPs refusing to forward packets from rival services)?

5. "Clear boundaries make law possible." How do Johnson and Post propose to resolve the inevitable "jurisdictional" disputes that will arise between "cyberspace" and the "real world?" How would they redress harm that takes place in an online venue against an absent party, such as defamation of a person who does not even own a computer?

6. In the offline context, it seems that jurisdiction is proper only if a person receives the "privileges and benefits" of the law of the forum. *World–Wide Volkswagen Corp. v. Woodson*, 444 U.S. 286, 295 (1980). Do Johnson and Post contend that any "Netizen" necessarily receives the privileges and benefits of the Internet and should therefore be subject to its jurisdiction (whatever "its jurisdiction" may mean)? On the other hand, it also seems that jurisdiction is proper only if it does not offend "traditional notions of fair play and substantial justice." *International Shoe Co. v. Washington*, 326 U.S. 310, 316 (1945) (quoting *Milliken v. Meyer*, 331 U.S. 457, 463 (1940)). How could any paradigm shift in response to the Internet possibly be considered "traditional?"

7. Barlow wrote: "The only law that all our constituent cultures would generally recognize is the Golden Rule. We hope we will be able to build our particular solutions on that basis." This appears to be a "lowest common denominator" approach to choice of law. Do you think that is preferable to other choice–of–law rules? Is it an inevitable choice, given Barlow's conception of cyber-

space? What other approach to choice of law could be employed
in an autonomous cyberspace?

III.B. Global Internet, Global Law: Uniform Procedures for Resolving Disputes over Cyberproperty

The "governance" of domain names by the Internet Corporation
for Assigned Names and Numbers ("ICANN") and its Uniform
Domain Name Dispute Resolution Policy ("UDRP") for the resolution of domain name disputes might be offered as examples of
the type of self–governance envisioned for cyberspace by Johnson,
Post, and Barlow.

BE CAREFUL WHAT YOU ASK FOR: RECONCILING A GLOBAL INTERNET AND LOCAL LAW (IV)
Jonathan Zittrain
Who Rules the Net?, Cato Institute, 2003

> Internet separatism lives on today primarily in debates about
> the application of state sales tax to out–of–state purchases
> made easy by the Internet. Unless pitched as infant industry
> subsidization, it is hard to imagine reasons why Internet–based
> purchases should effectively avoid tax while purchases con-
> summated in physical space do not. [ ] The most direct account
> to explain the perspective of those who seek continuing mora-
> toria on taxing Internet purchases is simply a hostility to gov-
> ernment regulation in general and taxes specifically. This is
> not an incoherent position; one might seek to prevent the "pris-
> tine" territory of the Net from being ruined by an encroach-
> ment of what one sees as irreversible overregulation in "real"
> space. But from the point of view of the dilemmas of jurisdic-
> tion and governance, it trades in one set of fault lines—those

between countries and other legal jurisdictions—for a new one, separating the physical and virtual worlds.

The most effective—if not beloved—global law scheme has so far proven to be conveniently centered on cyberspace-specific disputes, namely those over domain names. As part of its designation by the U.S. Department of Commerce to manage global domain name policy, the Internet Corporation for Assigned Names and Numbers devised a Uniform Dispute Resolution Policy for the adjudication of claims of improper registration of names in .com, .net, and .org. [ ] Operating wholly independently from any one nation's trademark laws, the UDRP neatly sidesteps many of the classic jurisdictional conundrums. A faraway or unknown domain name registrant had better step forward to defend against a claim that his or her domain name infringes someone else's rights, lest he or she lose the proceeding—and the name. Enforcement is made easy since no money or behavioral change is asked of the losing respondent—the registry is simply notified of the panel's decision and transfers control over the name to the complainant without any acquiescence required of the respondent. The substantive principles under which UDRP cases are decided are vague, requiring an assessment of the "rights" and "interests" of both parties to the dispute without specifying just how those rights should be recognized or under what sovereign's system. But this has not stopped thousands of UDRP cases from going forward, and the adoption of the UDRP system by a number of additional registries operating other generic and country-specific top level domains.

To be sure, use of the UDRP does not necessarily end legal wrangling—[for example], the U.S. Anticyber-squatting Consumer Protection Act provides its own mechanisms for seeking to complain about another's domain name registration, [ ] and any other number of trademark actions launched in countries willing to hear them could trump the UDRP's result, whether for complainant or respondent.[ ] . . .

Attempts to bind sovereigns' laws substantively more closely together in a world with burgeoning transborder activity continue, and to the extent they succeed some of the structural
jurisdictional tensions recede. International treaties and agreements have begun to cluster, if not fully unify, countries' practices on consumer protection, intellectual property, taxation,
and to some extent, privacy. But these shifts are incremental,
and often the inking of a treaty—or even, within the European
Union, the promulgation of a directive left for individual countries to implement—is only a starting point that tests individual countries' and cultures' mettle to actually enforce that
which has been abstractly agreed to.

FAST, CHEAP, AND OUT OF CONTROL: LESSONS FROM THE ICANN DISPUTE RESOLUTION PROCESS

Elizabeth G. Thornburg
6 J. Small & Emerging Bus. L. 191 (2002)

The Internet's domain name system is currently (since 1998)
administered by ICANN, a private, not-for-profit corporation,
under the authority of a series of understandings with the U.S.
Department of Commerce. One of ICANN's first assignments
was to adopt a dispute resolution policy to allow speedy and
inexpensive resolution of conflicts regarding rights to domain
names. ICANN approved its Uniform Domain Name Dispute
Resolution Policy (UDRP) and Rules for Uniform Domain Name
Dispute Resolution Policy on October 24, 1999, and they went
into effect on December 1, 1999. ICANN imposes this policy
on approved domain name registrars, and through them onto
all who acquire domain names.

One can see the superficial appeal of an ICANN-like
process to resolve international Internet disputes. First, it
applies globally; all disputes about top level domain names
ending in .com, .net, and .org are subject to this policy, no mat-

ter where in the world the parties reside or do business and no matter where the domain name holder registered the domain. This eliminates the tricky issue of personal jurisdiction over the domain name holder. It also manages to create a contractually–mandated private system for the benefit of noncontracting parties. Second, because the process does not require (or even allow) personal appearances by the parties, it minimizes geographic distance problems. Parties need not travel to participate in the process. Third, the UDRP attempts to overcome the choice of law problems raised by differences in national trademark laws by creating its own "law" in the ICANN policy. Finally, because ICANN has a contract with the company that controls the root server that assigns domain names, it has the power to enforce the arbitrators' decisions without the need to ask a court to enforce the judgment.

. . .

[T]he UDRP's operation is essentially a private process. ICANN itself is a private, nonprofit corporation whose policies are shaped both by governments and by influential private entities. ICANN has needed and still needs "the concurrence of every powerful party with an interest in domain name policy." In addition to governments (especially the U.S. and the European Union), this "concurrence" includes Internet engineering groups and trademark interests. ICANN "faces swift dispatch if it strays too far from the desires of . . . powerful corporate interests." ICANN developed its domain name dispute policy and the rules for implementing it with the input of these key groups. . . .

National interests have a role to play in the development of international solutions. Passing over them too quickly disserves a truly international solution by ignoring helpful laboratories of laws, failing to take advantage of developed democratic political structures that nation states (on the whole) provide, and ignoring the legitimate claims of nation states to (partial) legislative competence.

ICANN is a particularly problematic example because many believe that its formation and subsequent policies suffered from the over-influence of trademark holders, thus skewing the substantive and procedural rules in their favor. Similarly, the recent appointment of a task force to study the UDRP has been criticized as similarly stacked in favor of intellectual property interests and existing dispute resolution providers. A recent internal study of ICANN governance has recommended decreasing the number of at-large board members (who represent the online public), which has prompted further questions about ICANN's legitimacy.

. . .

Even if one overlooks the democratic deficit and accepts ICANN's authority to make law, the policy also allows the arbitrators to apply "any rules and principles of law . . . deem[ed] applicable." While this may seem like an innocent gap-filler, it has resulted in eclectic and unprincipled "choice of law" decisions as different arbitrators choose to apply various national laws or "principles of equity." This re-introduces the uncertainty about applicable law that the UDRP was created to prevent. It also exacerbates the differences among the decisions made by the unappealable arbitrators, who not only interpret the Policy but also choose when and how to supplement it with national law with virtually no guidance from the ICANN rules. This apparent need to consult national law, and, hence, the need for choice of law rules, may be a byproduct of trying to create enforceable private law in areas where national laws differ significantly. Any expansion of a UDRP-like process into areas with even greater international variation would cause even greater problems of this kind.

How does the issue of "legitimacy" in applying ICANN law create more difficulties than other state and foreign choice-of-law issues?

This problem could be minimized by allowing privatized, international rulemaking only in areas in which the international community has reached sufficient unanimity that resort to national law is not required. Otherwise, whether in the guise of creating substantive law or choice-of-law rules, the privatized body and its adjudicators would be making the kind of decisions better suited to democratic governments. Individual UDRP arbitrators should not be creating law by choosing or amalgamating possible national approaches.

. . .

Examining the UDRP from a distance also yields some more general lessons about the problems of creating privatized processes and the role that governments should play in their design and implementation. Any system that aspires to be fair must keep in mind the comparative power of the participants, and must include a way to monitor and enforce at least minimum standards.

Some Internet theory harkens back to the Net's early days as a relatively homogeneous band of fellow scientists and computer geeks. It posits that the rules of the Internet should be established through self-regulation that arises through the practices of the Internet community. With the addition of major commercial activity, the ideological hostility to government intervention shared by early Internet enthusiasts has now been bolstered by the free market vision of the commercial users. This law created by contract is alleged to be both more efficient and more fair than whatever a traditional government might require.

The ICANN experience, as well as the contracts of adhesion beginning to be used in e-commerce transactions, causes the concept of the Internet as a "community" of users regulating only themselves to collapse when commercial interests are at stake. As Professor Lemley notes: "[N]orms often operate among peers. If the society is divided into different groups—say, one group that always sells and another group that always buys—their desires and expectations from interaction may be so different that informal agreement is unlikely." In analyzing the privatized processes, we should abandon the fiction that these systems evolve naturally from the shared values of equally influential parties.

NOTES & QUESTIONS

1. Is the UDRP a good example of Johnson and Post's thinking? What are the exit options for a would–be domain name registrant who doesn't want to hew to the UDRP rules?

2. How satisfactory to trademark owners is a regime in which some domain names conform to the UDRP while others don't?

3. Do you agree that the emergence of e–commerce has altered the viability of the concept of the Internet as a "community" of users? Do you think that commercial transactions require a choice of law rule different from what Johnson and Post or Barlow described?

4. Barlow clearly disfavores any role in Internet governance for nation governments, but Thornburg insists that nations can and should play a role in developing methods of governance for the Net. Which position is more convincing?

DESIGNING NON–NATIONAL SYSTEMS: THE CASE OF THE UNIFORM DOMAIN NAME DISPUTE RESOLUTION POLICY

Laurence R. Helfer, Graeme B. Dinwoodie
43 Wm. and Mary L. Rev. 141 (October 2001)

[T]he question of whether policymakers should encourage the proliferation of non–national approaches to lawmaking and dispute settlement cannot be answered in the abstract. It depends instead on the methods used to legitimize non–national structures, which in turn hinges on such foundational issues as (1) the pace of non–national lawmaking and dispute settlement relative to their alternatives; (2) the design of checking mechanisms different from those currently found in the UDRP; (3) the degree to which non–national structures accommodate competing national values and interests; (4) the relationships between non–national structures and complementary or competing national and international ones; and (5) the substantive law that the system encompasses. . . .

. . .

We believe that some formal, organized rulemaking body, whether public or private, is essential to impose checking functions on [UDRP] panels, particularly if non-national legal norms will continue to serve at least in part as rules of decision for online domain name disputes. Existing treaty-based institutions are insufficient vehicles for the forms of lawmaking and dispute settlement demanded by a global and digital world. To be sure, such institutions tie the resultant rules more directly to the people that are governed through the national governments by whom such rules are negotiated. Treaty lawmaking, however, is too slow, and does not reflect the increasingly important interests that exist apart from (although partly overlapping with) the interests represented in national political units.

Clearly, we do not envisage (and the peoples of the world are not ready for) the creation of a world parliament to establish a direct link between the non-nationally governed and their non-national governors. Such a body is neither practical nor normatively compelling when (globalization notwithstanding) social identities and priorities remain linked in many important ways to nationality. But this does not mean that looser political structures of a non-national nature cannot be designed to complement national mechanisms. Nor does it imply that such structures cannot be nurtured to grow in line both with evolving social norms of community and with practical considerations. This growth, and the metrics for measuring its determinants, will appropriately be judged by the primary actors at the present stage of global political organization, namely the disaggregated national governments who are themselves subjected to pressures from individuals and private parties operating within and across nation states.

. . .

[W]e think it necessary to proceed simultaneously along two parallel tracks. On the one hand, we urge ICANN to shore up its non-national democracy deficit by introducing direct representation and voting structures. If such reforms can be accomplished, they would strengthen the allegiances between private non-national governors and the Internet stakeholders they seek to govern, without regard to nationality or national political loyalties. However, the example of the European Union's efforts to overcome its own democracy deficit shows that legitimizing supranational or non-national lawmaking structures through direct representation mechanisms is a slow and cumbersome process, one that may never fully supplant national political structures as proxies for the interests of the governed.

Therefore, as an additional strategy, we support the inclusion of national structures in the design or refurbishing of non-national lawmaking and dispute settlement systems on both pragmatic grounds and as a matter of principle. Pragmatically, facilitating input by the primary beneficiaries of the intellectual property system, namely the public, cannot be achieved without the input of national political structures. This is particularly true in the short term if non-national *lawmaking* is to continue at a relatively rapid clip while non-national *democratic mechanisms* evolve more slowly.

The inclusion of national structures is important for two reasons of principle. First, as one of us has argued elsewhere, actions taken in cyberspace have spillover effects off-line, where national governments have traditionally and uncontroversially exercised their authority within their own borders. For this reason, nations do have some legitimate claims to prescribe in cyberspace, and these must be accommodated in any non-national system.

Second, the addition of national structures into the lawmaking mix may diffuse public choice concerns. Some commentators have argued that international lawmaking structures of various stripes are especially susceptible to strategic pressures from certain interests groups, who have the resources and incentives to distort the lawmaking process in inefficient and substantively dubious ways. Indeed, the ICANN process has been heavily criticized in this regard. To be sure, national structures can also be strongly skewed by public choice pressures, but we believe that a divided non–national–national rulemaking competence (and the multiplicity of perspectives it engenders) will at worst not exacerbate public choice problems and may in fact check the ability of certain interest groups to achieve the dominance they might otherwise enjoy in a single lawmaking forum. . . .

. . .

Non–national lawmakers must also carefully consider the relationship between non–national systems and the rules and norms of public international law. Public international law can interact with non–national structures in at least three distinct ways: first, as a constraint on the subject matter of issues committed to the jurisdiction of non–national lawmakers; second, as a source of substantive rules to be applied in disputes between private parties adjudicated in non–national fora; and third, as a source of (depending on one's perspective) competition or inspiration for the creation of new legal rules relating to intellectual property rights. . . .

NOTES & QUESTIONS

1. Is a non–national approach, such as that taken in the governance of domain names, a useful or desirable model for other Internet governance issues?

2. Does the possibility of "exit" that Johnson and Post discussed reduce the significance of the "democratic deficit" that has impaired ICANN's credibility? Is "exit" a viable option for those who feel that their interests have not been adequately represented in Internet governance efforts?

III.C. Local Internet, Local Law: The Emergence of Physical Borders on the Internet

As a global network designed to operationally transcend, rather than respect, geographical lines, the Internet (as originally conceived and implemented) has been perceived as fundamentally ill–suited to local regulation based on geographic boundaries.

LAW AND BORDERS: THE RISE OF LAW IN CYBERSPACE
David R. Johnson and David G. Post
48 Stan. L. Rev. 1367 (1996)

> The rise of the global computer network is destroying the link between geographical location and: (1) the *power* of local governments to assert control over online behavior; (2) the *effects* of online behavior on individuals or things; (3) the *legitimacy* of the efforts of a local sovereign to enforce rules applicable to global phenomena; and (4) the ability of physical location to give *notice* of which sets of rules apply.
>
> . . .
>
> [The Internet] has no territorially–based boundaries, because the cost and speed of message transmission on the Net is almost entirely independent of physical location . . . . Location remains vitally important, but only location within a *virtual* space consisting of the "addresses" of the machines between which messages and information are routed.
>
> The system is indifferent to the *physical* location of those machines, and there is no necessary connection between an Internet address and a physical jurisdiction.
>
> Although a domain name, when initially assigned to a given machine, may be associated with a particular Internet Protocol

Recall the court's observation in ALA v. Pataki *that "the Internet is wholly insensitive to geographic distinctions." How does this observation relate to Johnson and Post's claims?*

address corresponding to the territory within which the machine is physically located (*e.g.*, a ".uk" domain name extension), the machine may move in physical space without any movement in the logical domain name space of the Net. Or, alternatively, the owner of the domain name might request that the name become associated with an entirely different machine, in a different physical location. Thus, a server with a ".uk" domain name may not necessarily be located in the United Kingdom, a server with a ".com" domain name may be anywhere, and users, generally speaking, are not even aware of the location of the server that stores the content that they read. Physical borders no longer can function as signposts informing individuals of the obligations assumed by entering into a new, legally significant place, because individuals are unaware of the existence of those borders as they move through virtual space.

Johnson and Post's article most notably describes the Internet as it was originally conceived and implemented by its founding engineers. Since their essay's debut in 1996, however, technology efforts aimed at enabling the introduction of geographical boundaries have been somewhat successful. The goal is to allow those who serve information on the Internet to be able to differentiate among users from respective locations. This has useful commercial implications; one could develop a "yellow pages" function by which nearby pizza parlors are automatically featured on a Web page requested by the user, or in a pop–up ad. It also has impact on the jurisdictional debate, since the "slowest ship in the convoy" objection then loses steam—France can demand of a content provider that its own citizens be limited from viewing certain information, without presenting that provider the Hobson's Choice of limiting everyone in the world from that material, even in areas where the material is legal.

The most common (and perhaps most promising) border–imposing technology involves "IP mapping," or the mapping of an Internet user's IP address to a geographic region. IP mapping is based on the fact that while, in theory, IP addresses need not correlate with geographic location at all, in practice, they do. Internet Service Providers ("ISPs") (through which most people access the Internet) usually assign IP addresses to their customers based on geographic location. A provider of IP mapping technology essentially assembles a massive directory of this information; IP addresses can be looked up in the directory and an associated geographic location provided, if available. Moreover, the directory can store other information about the user if the information is derivable from the IP address, *e.g.*, the identity of his or her ISP and the bandwidth of his or her Internet connection.

IP mapping is not solely a science. It often requires business relationships with ISPs to uncover geographic data on their customers; and a host of technological issues—largely a result of the fact that, fundamentally, the Internet was not designed to preserve geographic information—can make the data highly unreliable. The imperfect character of the technology is evident in the product descriptions crafted by its providers. For example, Quova, one of the leading developers of this technology, describes its GeoPoint product as follows:

> Quova's flagship GeoPoint service is an enterprise-class geolocation solution that leverages a combination of cutting-edge technology and unrivalled human expertise to instantly and accurately determine the real-world location of a Web site visitor—down to the country, region, state or city level—as well as critical routing and connection data. GeoPoint performs by mapping the 1.4 billion routable IP addresses on the Internet using proprietary algorithms, a worldwide network of servers and expert analysis, through which GeoPoint data is processed and analyzed.
>
> . . .
>
> The ability of Quova's GeoPoint to instantly determine the real-world location of a Web site visitor has proven a business-critical solution for a variety of applications, including:

Fraud Detection—By comparing the online visitor's geographic location and routing data to the registered address on the account,

. . .

Digital Rights Management—Digital content providers and online gaming enterprises use GeoPoint to instantly determine whether each customer is in a location where the proposed transaction can be legally completed. . .

Regulatory Compliance—Strict new "Know Your Customer" laws threaten global trade companies with sanctions, fines and criminal charges for trading with restricted parties, and Quova's geolocation helps protect them from regulatory violations;

. . .

Network Security—Real-time geolocation data can be leveraged as a network watchdog to provide a first-alert intrusion alarm based on the location of the potential intruder, as well as highly effective forensic data used by multiple government investigatory agencies to track online offenders.

. . .

The internationally-respected auditor Pricewaterhouse-Coopers . . . audited test results for Quova's geolocation data quality using independent third-party data sets of actual Web users. Quova's country-level accuracy was measured at 99.9% and US state-level accuracy at 94.0%.

Though imperfect, IP mapping can be very effective, particularly when users of the technology do not require a high degree of specificity or granularity in defining geographic locations. IP mapping can very accurately predict the country from which a viewer accesses a Web site, but it might fail to reliably predict his or her town.

Naturally, IP mapping is often deployed by Web site operators for a variety of commercial reasons. Often, tailoring a marketing message to a user on the basis of his or her geographic location can be very effective. Similarly, companies often employ IP mapping in order to provide accurate shipping and availability information on products on the basis of a user's location without requiring that user to explicitly divulge his or her location. In the context of our discussion of jurisdiction on the Internet, the most notable use of the technology is, naturally, using IP mapping to guarantee compliance with the regulations of the sovereign state in which a user resides. Given the ability to know the geographic location of its viewers, a company can construct its Web site so as to respond differently to viewers in different geographic regions as a function of the respective laws of those regions. Virtgame.com, in its description of its eBorder Controls product, explains, for example: "Virtgame.com's eBorder Controls ensure that Internet and closed–loop content and activity . . . meet specified geographical distribution and legal restrictions."

NOTES & QUESTIONS

1. Would IP mapping, or even hypothetically "perfect" IP mapping, effectively avoid the special jurisdictional issues created by the Internet?

2. While IP mapping is the first step in one approach to imposing borders in cyberspace, there are several other approaches that could be employed. Some of these approaches are attempts to recreate the geography that is avoided by the current Internet technology, but others aim to impose borders based on user traits, such as age, that might be relevant to the legality of a user viewing material on a site. Some possible approaches include: asking users to indicate what their location is or asking for some other information that would effectively indicate location (e.g., telephone area code); requiring users to click a box to verify some fact (e.g., age or location); requesting credit card information to verify age; or applying password protection to a site so that only

authenticated, registered users can gain access. One technology that is already being rolled out in cellular telephones that could be expanded to other Internet–access devices (such as PCs or handheld computers) is satellite GPS (global positioning systems). GPS can be used in computers, as well as in other devices such as phones or cars, to indicate and authenticate location. This is perhaps most directly useful in cell phone applications to enable effective functioning of the 911 emergency response system to cell phone calls, but it could be just as effective at verifying an Internet user's location to determine what sites the user may access. A slightly different approach might use something like top–level domain name "zones," such as a .xxx or a .kids domain, where the content available in that domain is limited to content that fits some defined category. Still another approach might employ filters to block access to specific Web sites as harmful speech.

3. The cases that are included in this section offer some examples of other border–imposing technologies. In *ICraveTV*, the defendants implemented a border–imposing technology that consisted of requiring a visitor to the site to state his or her phone number; any number that included a Canadian area code enabled access to the site while U.S. area codes were turned away. The site had no way of verifying that the phone number entered actually belonged to the visitor. The measure was deemed ineffective because it was so easy for a visitor to the site to feign Canadian residence and gain access. In *Yahoo! France*, the French court described various methods Yahoo! could use to determine whether a given visitor to its site was from France. That court concluded that a combination of geographic determination based on IP addresses and declaration of nationality would be sufficiently accurate to enable Yahoo! to avoid allowing French nationals access to offending portions of its site.

4. To be sure, if Internet users were so inclined, they would probably not have too much trouble avoiding the limits imposed by IP mapping technologies. By routing their Net access through a proxy that masked the IP address of their initial access point they could fool most zoning programs into thinking they were

from somewhere else. But the fact that border–imposing technology might not be fail–safe does not mean that it would not be more or less effective. The truth is that most users probably would not try to mask their IP addresses; though it may not be extremely difficult to accomplish, it would require extra effort and some additional knowledge. A big part of the enforcement game is won by asking suppliers of content to demand such extreme measures by their customers; if the suppliers' demand is genuinely imposed, they should be able to avoid liability should their customers resort to those extreme measures.

In fact, the difference between the courts' satisfaction with border–imposing technologies in *ICraveTV* and *Yahoo! France* might be attributable in part to this balancing of fault. In the *ICraveTV* case, the wrong at issue was the unauthorized transmission of protected material; it did not really matter where the recipients of the material were located—the responsible party was ICraveTV. ICraveTV could not avoid responsibility for people in the United States accessing its system just because it imposed some meager enforcement measure; assuming it was legal for ICraveTV to stream the programs to customers in Canada, if the company had employed some more reliable method of blocking access to persons outside of Canada, it might have avoided a restraining order. In the case of *Yahoo! France*, on the other hand, not only was it illegal for Yahoo! to display Nazi images and memorabilia to people in France; it was also illegal for people in France to view the material. If Yahoo! made a reasonable effort to prevent access to the illegal materials by people in France, such as by employing IP mapping technology and requiring an affirmative representation by users that they were not in France, Yahoo! could escape liability, even if some users where able to get through to the prohibited material. In that case, those users would themselves be liable.

III.D. Local Internet, Local Law: From Physical Borders to Broader Zoning on the Internet

Zoning regulations restrict owners of land in its use. They empower localities to implement strategies that maximize the use and value of land. They might guarantee, for example, that nobody can lawfully construct a skyscraper in the middle of a residential neighborhood of single–family homes or that nobody will locate a home along a strip of shopping plazas. These regulations serve not only the functions of civic planning, but also to protect investments made in land by providing a measure of certainty as to the character of surrounding lands.

Zoning regulations also play a valuable role in enforcing community standards. Strict regulations as to where adult entertainment establishments can locate, for example, ensure that members of the community can avoid such establishments. Parents can rest assured that their children will not walk by a topless bar on their way to school.

Earlier in this chapter, we considered the idea that the architecture of the Internet—though hostile to regulation in its current form—is as up for grabs as are the laws that regulate its use. Changes can be made to the underlying technology that drives the Internet that can dramatically alter its characteristics.

The practice of zoning in the physical world presents an intriguing metaphor for a highly–regulable vision of the Internet's architecture. This zoning metaphor presupposes an imposition of physical boundaries on the Internet's architecture. We will explore the concept of Internet zoning more fully below. First, we consider a real–world zoning case involving the physical location of a pornographic Web site.

At issue in *Voyeur Dorm v. City of Tampa*, 265 F.3d 1232 (11th Cir. 2001), was an alleged violation of Tampa's City Code based on the district court's characterization of Voyeur Dorm as an adult entertainment facility. Voyeur Dorm is a company that operates a Web site that features live video transmission of the goings–on in a house in Tampa, Florida. Occupying the house are 25 to 30 women who have agreed to be filmed for entertainment purposes. Voyeur Dorm charges subscription fees for Internet users to visit the site and watch the film footage that is available there. The city alleged that Voyeur Dorm violated the city's zoning ordinance that prohibited use of a residential location for adult entertainment; adult entertainment was defined in the ordinance as "Any [sic] premises . . . on which is offered to members of the public or any person, for a consideration, entertainment featuring or in any way including specified sexual activities." The city argued (and the district court found) that the ordinance did not require that the public actually be on the premises viewing the adult entertainment. Voyeur Dorm countered, and the appellate court agreed, that the ordinance applied to locations or premises where adult entertainment is actually offered to the public, and since the public was not allowed on the premises in question that Voyeur Dorm was not in violation of the zoning ordinance. "Here, the audience or consumers of the adult entertainment do not go to [the house] or congregate anywhere else in Tampa to enjoy the entertainment. Indeed, the public offering occurs over the Internet in 'virtual space.'"

The concept of zoning as extended to the Internet has more profound implications than simply regulating Internet businesses based on their physical location in a zone. While the most intuitive kind of "cyber–zoning" might be the use of dedicated top–level domains to segregate different types of content, any border–imposing technology coupled with restrictions as to what location, age, or other characteristic is required for access can create zones.

THE ZONES OF CYBERSPACE
Lawrence Lessig .
48 Stan. L. Rev. 1403 (1996)

. . . [We] must say something about what cyberspace will become, and it is here that I think Johnson and Post are most ambitious, one might say romantic, while I am firmly skeptical. Their picture is of a democracy in cyberspace—of a world of cybercitizens deciding on the laws that will apply to them, and a claim that this more perfect democracy deserves respect. The separation that they argue for comes then from the respect that we owe this autonomy.

This is a hope built on a picture of cyberspace as it is just now. As it is just now, cyberspace is such a place of relative freedom. The technologies of control are relatively crude. Not that there is no control. Cyberspace is not anarchy. But that control is exercised through the ordinary tools of human regulation—through social norms, and social stigma; through peer pressure, and reward. How this happens is an amazing question—how people who need never meet can establish and enforce a rich set of social norms is a question that will push theories of social norm development far. But no one who has lived any part of her life in this space as it is just now can doubt that this is a space filled with community, and with the freedom that the imperfections of community allows.

This is changing. Cyberspace is changing. And to understand what this change could be, we must think again about the very nature of cyberspace itself—more particularly, about the nature of how cyberspace regulates itself.

Think of how a community regulates itself in real space. In real space, when the state wants to regulate something—say littering—the state threatens, or cajoles, through prisons or fines or furry little animals on TV, to induce people to internalize this norm against littering. If the state succeeds, behavior changes. But its success depends upon individuals internalizing what the state requires. Between the norm and the behavior sought is a human being, mediating whether to conform or not. Lots of times, for lots of laws, the choice is not to conform. Regardless of what the law says, it is an individual who decides whether to conform.

Regulation in cyberspace is, or can be, different. If the regulator wants to induce a certain behavior, she need not threaten, or cajole, to inspire the change. She need only change the code—the software that defines the terms upon which the individual gains access to the system, or uses assets on the system. If she wants to limit trespass on a system, she need not rely simply on a law against trespass; she can implement a system of passwords. If she wants to limit the illegal use of copyrighted material, she need not rely on the threat of copyright law; she can encrypt the copyrighted material so only those intended to have access will have access. Always in principle, and increasingly in practice, there is a code (as in software) to assure what the code (as in law) demands, which means always in principle and increasingly in practice, law is inscribed in the code.

Code is an efficient means of regulation. But its perfection makes it something different. One obeys these laws as code not because one should; one obeys these laws as code because one can do nothing else. There is no choice about whether to yield to the demand for a password; one complies if one wants to enter the system. In the well implemented system, there is no civil disobedience. Law as code is a start to the perfect technology of justice.

It is not this just now. Just now the architecture of cyberspace is quite imperfect. Indeed, what is central about its present architecture is the anarchy that it preserves. Some see this anarchy as inherent in the space, as unavoidable. But this anarchy is just a consequence of the present design. In its present design, cyberspace is open, and uncontrolled; regulation is achieved through social forces much like the social forms that

How does Lessig's conception of code relate to ICANN's control over the domain names system?

regulate real space. It is now unzoned: Borders are not boundaries; they divide one system from another just as Pennsylvania is divided from Ohio. The essence of cyberspace today is the search engine—tools with which one crosses an infinite space, to locate, and go to, the stuff one wants. The space today is open, but only because it is made that way. Or because we made it that way. (For whatever is true about society, at least cyberspace is socially constructed.)

It could be made to be different, and my sense is that it is. The present architecture of cyberspace is changing. If there is one animating idea behind the kinds of reforms pursued both in the social and economic spheres in cyberspace, it is the idea to increase the sophistication of the architecture in cyberspace, to facilitate boundaries rather than borders. It is the movement to bring zoning to cyberspace . . . .

We are just at the beginning of this change. Zoning will replace the present wilderness of cyberspace, and this zoning will be achieved through code—a tool, as Johnson and Post suggest, more perfect than any equivalent tool of zoning in real space. The architecture of cyberspace will in principle allow for perfect zoning—a way perfectly to exclude those who would cross boundaries . . . .

One might well say that this movement to more perfect zoning is just what "the people want." But want here is complex. They want control over what their kids get access to; they want control over who "takes" their intellectual "property." They want to control what their citizens read. All these "theys" have lots to gain from the architecture that cyberspace is becoming, and we are a lot of these "theys." Commerce is built on property, and property depends upon boundaries. What possible reason could there be to question the value of clear borders?

But we might nonetheless find reason to be skeptical, or at least reason to raise doubts. . . . As important as the nature of these newly zoned spaces is, more important is who is designing them. They are the construction, as Johnson and Post describe, of "engineers." Engineers write the code; the code defines the architectures, and the architectures define what is possible within a certain social space. No process of democracy defines this social space, save if the market is a process of democracy.

This might not be so bad, assuming that there are enough places to choose from, and given that it is cyberspace, the places to choose from could be many, and the costs of exit are quite low. Even so, note the trend: the progression away from democratic control. We will stand in relation to these places of cyberspace as we stand in relation to the commodities of the market: one more place of unending choice; but one less place where we, collectively, have a role in constructing the choices that we have.

ASHCROFT V. ACLU
535 U.S. 564 (2002)

[Justice Thomas delivered the opinion of the Court.]

This case presents the narrow question whether the Child Online Protection Act's ("COPA" or "Act") use of "community standards" to identify "material that is harmful to minors" violates the First Amendment. We hold that this aspect of COPA does not render the statute facially unconstitutional.

. . .

Congress first attempted to protect children from exposure to pornographic material on the Internet by enacting the Communications Decency Act of 1996 (CDA), 110 Stat. 133. The CDA prohibited the knowing transmission over the Internet of obscene or indecent messages to any recipient under 18 years of age. See 47 U.S.C. § 223(a). It also forbade any individual from knowingly sending over or displaying on the Internet certain "patently offensive" material in a manner available to persons under 18 years of age. See § 223(d). The prohibition specifically extended to "any comment, request, suggestion, proposal, image, or other communication that, in context, depict[ed] or describ[ed], in terms patently offensive as measured by contemporary community standards, sexual or excretory activities or organs." § 223(d)(1).

. . .

. . . [I]n *Reno v. American Civil Liberties Union*, we held that the CDA's regulation of indecent transmissions, see § 223(a), and the display of patently offensive material, see § 223(d), ran afoul of the First Amendment. We concluded that "the CDA lack[ed] the precision that the First Amendment requires when a statute regulates the content of speech" because, "[i]n order to deny minors access to potentially harmful speech, the CDA effectively suppress[ed] a large amount of speech that adults ha[d] a constitutional right to receive and to address to one another." 521 U.S., at 874, 117 S. Ct. 2329.

. . .

After our decision in *Reno v. American Civil Liberties Union*, Congress explored other avenues for restricting minors' access to pornographic material on the Internet. In particular, Congress passed and the President signed into law the Child Online Protection Act, 112 Stat. 2681–736 (codified in 47 U.S.C. § 231 (1994 ed., Supp. V)). COPA prohibits any person from "knowingly and with knowledge of the character of the material, in interstate or foreign commerce by means of the World Wide Web, mak[ing] any communication for commercial purposes that is available to any minor and that includes any material that is harmful to minors." 47 U.S.C. § 231(a)(1).

Apparently responding to our objections to the breadth of the CDA's coverage, Congress limited the scope of COPA's coverage in at least three ways. First, while the CDA applied to communications over the Internet as a whole, including, for example, e-mail messages, COPA applies only to material displayed on the World Wide Web. Second, unlike the CDA, COPA covers only communications made "for commercial purposes." *Id.* And third, while the CDA prohibited "indecent" and "patently offensive" communications, COPA restricts only the narrower category of "material that is harmful to minors." *Id.*

Drawing on the three-part test for obscenity set forth in *Miller v. California*, 413 U.S. 15, 93 S.Ct. 2607, 37 L. Ed. 2d 419 (1973), COPA defines "material that is harmful to minors" as:

> "any communication, picture, image, graphic image file, article, recording, writing, or other matter of any kind that is obscene or that—

> "(A) the average person, applying contemporary community standards, would find, taking the material as a whole and with respect to minors, is designed to appeal to, or is designed to pander to, the prurient interest;

> "(B) depicts, describes, or represents, in a manner patently offensive with respect to minors, an actual or simulated sexual act or sexual contact, an actual or simulated normal or perverted sexual act, or a lewd exhibition of the genitals or post-pubescent female breast; and

> "(C) taken as a whole, lacks serious literary, artistic, political, or scientific value for minors." 47 U.S.C. § 231(e)(6).

Like the CDA, COPA also provides affirmative defenses to those subject to prosecution under the statute. An individual may qualify for a defense if he, "in good faith, has restricted access by minors to material that is harmful to minors—(A) by requiring the use of a credit card, debit account, adult access code, or adult personal identification number; (B) by accepting a digital certificate that verifies age; or (C) by any other reasonable measures that are feasible under available technology." § 231(c)(1). Persons violating COPA are subject to both civil and criminal sanctions. A civil penalty of up to $50,000 may be imposed for each violation of the statute. Criminal penalties consist of up to six months in prison and/or a maximum fine of $50,000. An additional fine of $50,000 may be imposed for any intentional violation of the statute. § 231(a).

One month before COPA was scheduled to go into effect, respondents filed a lawsuit challenging the constitutionality of the statute in the United States District Court for the Eastern District of Pennsylvania. Respondents are a diverse group of organizations, most of which maintain their own Web sites. While the vast majority of content on their Web sites is available for free, respondents all derive income from their sites. Some, for example, sell advertising that is displayed on their Web sites, while others either sell goods directly over their sites or charge artists for the privilege of posting material. 31 F. Supp.2d, at 487. All respondents either post or have members that post sexually oriented material on the Web. *Id.*, at 480. Respondents' Web sites contain "resources on obstetrics, gynecology, and sexual health; visual art and poetry; resources designed for gays and lesbians; information about books and stock photographic images offered for sale; and online magazines." *Id.*, at 484.

In their complaint, respondents alleged that, although they believed that the material on their Web sites was valuable for adults, they feared that they would be prosecuted under COPA because some of that material "could be construed as 'harmful to minors' in some communities. . . ."

[A majority of the Court agreed that COPA's use of "community standards" does not by itself run afoul of the First Amendment, but the Justices split on the appropriate rationale behind their decision and wrote several concurring opinions. Justice Thomas, joined by Chief Justice Rehnquist and Justice Scalia, wrote the following.]

In *Hamling v. United States*, 418 U.S. 87, 94 S.Ct. 2887, 41 L.Ed.2d 590 (1974), this Court considered the constitutionality of applying community standards to the determination of whether material is obscene under 18 U.S.C. § 1461, the federal statute prohibiting the mailing of obscene material. Although this statute does not define obscenity, the petitioners in *Hamling* were tried and convicted under the definition of obscenity set forth in *Book Named "John Cleland's Memoirs of a Woman of Pleasure" v. Attorney General of Mass.*, 383 U.S. 413, 86 S.Ct. 975, 16 L.Ed.2d 1 (1966), which included both a "prurient interest" requirement and a requirement that prohibited material be "'utterly without redeeming social value.'" *Hamling, supra*, at 99, 94 S.Ct. 2887 . . . .

Like respondents here, the dissenting opinion in *Hamling* argued that it was unconstitutional for a federal statute to rely on community standards to regulate speech. Justice Brennan maintained that "[n]ational distributors choosing to send their products in interstate travels [would] be forced to cope with the community standards of every hamlet into which their goods [might] wander." 418 U.S., at 144, 94 S.Ct. 2887. As a result, he claimed that the inevitable result of this situation would be "debilitating self-censorship that abridges the First Amendment rights of the people." *Id.*

This Court, however, rejected Justice Brennan's argument that the federal mail statute unconstitutionally compelled speakers choosing to distribute materials on a national basis to tailor their messages to the least tolerant community: "The fact that distributors of allegedly obscene materials may be subjected to varying community standards in the various federal judicial districts into which they transmit the materials does not render a federal statute unconstitutional." *Id.,* at 106, 94 S. Ct. 2887.

Fifteen years later, *Hamling*'s holding was reaffirmed in *Sable Communications of California, Inc. v. Federal Communications Commission,* et al., 492 U.S. 115, 109 S. Ct. 2829, 106 L. Ed. 2d 93 (1989). Sable addressed the constitutionality of 47 U.S.C. § 223(b) (1982 ed., Supp. V), a statutory provision prohibiting the use of telephones to make obscene or indecent communications for commercial purposes. The petitioner in that case, a "dial-a-porn" operator, challenged, in part, that portion of the statute banning obscene phone messages. Like respondents here, the "dial-a-porn" operator argued that reliance on community standards to identify obscene material impermissibly compelled "message senders . . . to tailor all their messages to the least tolerant community." 492 U.S., at 124, 109 S. Ct. 2829. Relying on *Hamling*, however, this Court once again rebuffed this attack on the use of community standards in a federal statute of national scope: "There is no constitutional barrier under *Miller* to prohibiting communications that are obscene in some communities under local standards even though they are not obscene in others. *If Sable's audience is comprised of different communities with different local standards, Sable ultimately bears the burden of complying with the prohibition on obscene messages.*" 492 U.S., at 125–126, 109 S. Ct. 2829 (emphasis added).

The Court of Appeals below concluded that *Hamling* and *Sable* "are easily distinguished from the present case" because in both of those cases "the defendants had the ability to control the distribution of controversial material with respect to the geographic communities into which they released it" whereas "Web publishers have no such comparable control." 217 F.3d, at 175–176. In neither *Hamling* nor *Sable*, however, was the speaker's ability to target the release of material into particular geographic areas integral to the legal analysis. In *Hamling*, the ability to limit the distribution of material to targeted communities was not mentioned, let alone relied upon, and in *Sable*, a "dial–a–porn" operator's ability to screen incoming calls from particular areas was referenced only as a supplemental point, see 492 U.S., at 125, 109 S. Ct. 2829. In the latter case, this Court made no effort to evaluate how burdensome it would have been for dial–a–porn operators to tailor their messages to callers from thousands of different communities across the Nation, instead concluding that the burden of complying with the statute rested with those companies. See *Id.,* at 126, 109 S. Ct. 2829.

While Justice KENNEDY and Justice STEVENS question the applicability of this Court's community standards jurisprudence to the Internet, we do not believe that the medium's "unique characteristics" justify adopting a different approach than that set forth in *Hamling* and *Sable*. . . . If a publisher chooses to send its material into a particular community, this Court's jurisprudence teaches that it is the publisher's responsibility to abide by that community's standards. The publisher's burden does not change simply because it decides to distribute its material to every community in the Nation. . . . Nor does it change because the publisher may wish to speak only to those in a "community where avant garde culture is the norm," . . . but nonetheless utilizes a medium that transmits its speech from coast to coast. If a publisher wishes for its material to be judged only by the standards of particular communities, then it need only take the simple step of utilizing a medium that enables it to target the release of its material into those communities.

. . .

Justice O'CONNOR, concurring in part and concurring in the judgment.

I agree with the plurality that even if obscenity on the Internet is defined in terms of local community standards, respondents have not shown that the Child Online Protection Act (COPA) is overbroad solely on the basis of the variation in the standards of different communities. . . . I write separately to express my views on the constitutionality and desirability of adopting a national standard for obscenity for regulation of the Internet.

. . . [G]iven Internet speakers' inability to control the geographic location of their audience, expecting them to bear the burden of controlling the recipients of their speech, as we did in *Hamling* and *Sable*, may be entirely too much to ask, and would potentially suppress an inordinate amount of expression. . . . For these reasons, adoption of a national standard is necessary in my view for any reasonable regulation of Internet obscenity.

. . .

To be sure, the Court in *Miller* also stated that a national standard might be "unascertainable," 413 U.S., at 31, 93 S. Ct. 2607, and "[un]realistic." *Id.,* at 32, 93 S. Ct. 2607. But where speech on the Internet is concerned, I do not share that skepticism. It is true that our Nation is diverse, but many local communities encompass a similar diversity . . . . Moreover, the existence of the Internet, and its facilitation of national dialogue, has itself made jurors more aware of the views of adults in other parts of the United States. Although jurors asked to evaluate the obscenity of speech based on a national standard will inevitably base their assessments to some extent on their experience of their local communities, I agree with Justice BREYER that the lesser degree of variation that would result is inherent in the jury system and does not necessarily pose a First Amendment problem . . . . In my view, a national standard is not only constitutionally permissible, but also reasonable.

Justice BREYER, concurring in part and concurring in the judgment.

I write separately because I believe that Congress intended the statutory word "community" to refer to the Nation's adult community taken as a whole, not to geographically separate local areas. The statutory language does not explicitly describe the specific "community" to which it refers. It says only that the "average person, applying contemporary community standards," must find that the "material as a whole and with respect to minors, is designed to appeal to, or is designed to pander to, the prurient interest . . . ." 47 U.S.C. § 231(e)(6) (1994 ed., Supp. V).

In the statute's legislative history, however, Congress made clear that it did not intend this ambiguous statutory phrase to refer to separate standards that might differ significantly among different communities. The relevant House of Representatives Report says:

"The Committee recognizes that the applicability of community standards in the context of the Web is controversial, *but understands it as an 'adult' standard, rather than a 'geographic' standard, and one that is reasonably constant among adults in America with respect to what is suitable for minors.*" H.R. Rep. No. 105–775, 28 (1998) (emphasis added).

This statement, reflecting what apparently was a uniform view within Congress, makes clear that the standard, and the relevant community, is national and adult.

. . . To read the statute as adopting the community standards of every locality in the United States would provide the most puritan of communities with a heckler's Internet veto affecting the rest of the Nation. . . .

Justice KENNEDY, with whom Justice SOUTER and Justice GINSBURG join, concurring in the judgment.

. . .

The economics and technology of Internet communication differ in important ways from those of telephones and mail. Paradoxically, as the District Court found, it is easy and cheap to reach a worldwide audience on the Internet, see 31 F. Supp. 2d, at 482, but expensive if not impossible to reach a geographic subset. *Id.,* at 484. A Web publisher in a community where avant garde culture is the norm may have no desire to reach a national market; he may wish only to speak to his neighbors; nevertheless, if an eavesdropper in a more traditional, rural community chooses to listen in, there is nothing the publisher can do. As a practical matter, COPA makes the eavesdropper the arbiter of propriety on the Web. And it is no answer to say that the speaker should "take the simple step of utilizing a [different] medium." . . . "Our prior decisions have voiced particular concern with laws that foreclose an entire medium of expression . . . . [T]he danger they pose to the freedom of speech is readily apparent—by eliminating a common means of speaking, such measures can suppress too much speech." *City of Ladue v. Gilleo*, 512 U.S. 43, 55, 114 S. Ct. 2038, 129 L. Ed. 2d 36 (1994).

. . .

We cannot know whether variation in community standards renders the Act substantially overbroad without first assessing the extent of the speech covered and the variations in community standards with respect to that speech.

. . .

. . . [I]t is essential to answer the vexing question of what it means to evaluate Internet material "as a whole," 47 U.S.C. § § 231(e)(6)(A), (C), when everything on the Web is connected to everything else. As a general matter, "[t]he artistic merit of a work does not depend on the presence of a single explicit scene . . . . [T]he First Amendment requires that redeeming value be judged by considering the work as a whole. Where the scene is part of the narrative, the work itself does not for this reason become obscene, even though the scene in isolation might be offensive." *Ashcroft v. Free Speech Coalition*, ante, 535 U.S. 248, 122 S. Ct. 1389. COPA appears to respect this principle by requiring that the material be judged "as a whole," both as to its prurient appeal, § 231(e)(6)(A), and as to its social value, § 231(e)(6)(C). It is unclear, however, what constitutes the denominator—that is, the material to be taken as a whole—in the context of the World Wide Web. See 31 F. Supp. 2d, at 483 ("Although information on the Web is contained in individual computers, the fact that each of these computers is connected to the Internet through World Wide Web protocols allows all of the information to become part of a single body of knowledge"); *Id.*, at 484 ("From a user's perspective, [the World Wide Web] may appear to be a single, integrated system"). Several of the respondents operate extensive Web sites, some of which include only a small amount of material that might run afoul of the Act. The Attorney General contended that these respondents had nothing to fear from COPA, but the District Court disagreed, noting that the Act prohibits communication that "includes" any material harmful to minors. § 231(a)(1). In the District Court's view, "it logically follows that [COPA] would apply to any Web site that contains only some harmful to minors material." *Id.*, at 480. The denominator question is of crucial significance to the coverage of the Act. . . .

Justice STEVENS, dissenting.

Appeals to prurient interests are commonplace on the Internet, as in older media. Many of those appeals lack serious value for minors as well as adults. Some are offensive to certain viewers but welcomed by others. For decades, our cases have recognized that the standards for judging their acceptability vary from viewer to viewer and from community to community. Those cases developed the requirement that communications should be protected if they do not violate contemporary community standards. In its original form, the community standard provided a shield for communications that are offensive only to the least tolerant members of society. Thus, the Court "has emphasized on more than one occasion that a principal concern in requiring that a judgment be made on the basis of 'contemporary community standards' is to assure that the material is judged neither on the basis of each juror's personal opinion, nor by its effect on a particularly sensitive or insensitive person or group." *Hamling v. United States*, 418 U.S. 87, 107, 94 S. Ct. 2887, 41 L. Ed. 2d 590 (1974). In the context of the Internet, however, community standards become a sword, rather than a shield. If a prurient appeal is offensive in a puritan village, it may be a crime to post it on the World Wide Web.

. . .

COPA not only restricts speech that is made available to the general public, it also covers a medium in which speech cannot be segregated to avoid communities where it is likely to be considered harmful to minors. The Internet presents a unique forum for communication because information, once posted, is accessible everywhere on the network at once. The speaker cannot control access based on the location of the listener, nor can it choose the pathways through which its speech is transmitted. By approving the use of community standards in this context, Justice THOMAS endorses a construction of COPA that has "the intolerable consequence of denying some sections of the country access to material, there deemed acceptable, which in others might be considered offensive to prevailing community standards of decency." *Manual Enterprises, Inc. v. Day*, 370 U.S. 478, 488, 82 S. Ct. 1432, 8 L. Ed. 2d 639 (1962).

. . .

In the context of most other media, using community standards to differentiate between permissible and impermissible speech has two virtues. As mentioned above, community standards originally served as a shield to protect speakers from the least tolerant members of society. By aggregating values at the community level, the *Miller* test eliminated the outliers at both ends of the spectrum and provided some predictability as to what constitutes obscene speech. But community standards also serve as a shield to protect audience members, by allowing people to self-sort based on their preferences. Those who abhor and those who tolerate sexually explicit speech can seek out like-minded people and settle in communities that share their views on what is acceptable for themselves and their children. This sorting mechanism, however, does not exist in cyberspace; the audience cannot self-segregate. As a result, in the context of the Internet this shield also becomes a sword, because the community that wishes to live without certain material rids not only itself, but the entire Internet, of the offending speech. . . .

THE NEWNESS OF NEW TECHNOLOGY
Monroe E. Price
22 Cardozo L. Rev. 1885 (2001)

The opinion of Justice O'Connor in *Reno* illustrates the problem of adjusting to metaphors while assessing a new technology. She relates a wish to think of the Internet as a land, inhabited by a number of institutions, some of whom are purveyors of indecent material. For her, the relevant ways of thinking about the law are to consider the applicability of legal analogies. In her opinion she looks, especially, toward decisions concerning the more physical world of bookstores and their locations. There, the Court has endorsed the establishment of "adult zones," specified physical sites that deal in pornographic materials and that can be segregated to particular parts of towns and cities, thus removed from children. By relying on the notion that this is a "zoning case"—which is itself a vision of cyberspace—she makes her own leap, coping with the new but well within existing modes of fashioning principles.

But Justice O'Connor demonstrates that she cannot be sure the analogy would work. Is zoning in cyberspace the same as zoning in the physical world? Justice O'Connor expresses doubts whether the received doctrine respecting speech-related zoning—rules that she finds acceptable in their traditional application to street corners in cities—should apply in cyberspace. The image of the adult bookshop, with its masked windows, the forbidden entry, the lonely monitor working into the night, translates into cyberspace only with difficulty. "Before today," Justice O'Connor writes, there was no reason to question the approach of zoning, for before the Internet case "the Court has previously only considered law that operated in the physical world, a world with two characteristics that make it possible to create 'adult zones': geography and identity." This new layer of abstraction is what forces the rethinking of the Constitution and basic principles in the world of cyberspace. Thus, Justice O'Connor retains her commitment to the architecture of her past constitutional doctrine, but recognizes the complexity of extending it to the new technologies.

III.E. A Case on the Cusp of a New Internet: Yahoo! France Part II, The View From France

On May 22, 2000, the Tribunal de Grande Instance de Paris issued a preliminary injunction against Yahoo!, Inc., an American company, in a case brought against Yahoo! and Yahoo! France by two nonprofit organizations dedicated to eliminating anti–Semitism. In France, the display of objects representing symbols of Nazi ideology is a violation of the penal code. In response to the offering on a Yahoo! auction site of Nazi memorabilia the French groups sought to prevent Yahoo! from making available in France any Web pages stored on Yahoo!'s servers that auctioned Nazi objects or presented any materials containing Nazi sympathy or Holocaust denial.

The May order contained the following terms:

> We order the company YAHOO! Inc. to take all measures to dissuade and make impossible any access via Yahoo.com to the auction service for Nazi objects and to any other site or service that may be construed as constituting an apology for Nazism or contesting the reality of Nazi crimes;
>
> We order the company YAHOO! FRANCE to warn any surfer visiting Yahoo.fr, even before use is made of the link enabling him or her to proceed with searches on Yahoo.com, that if the result of any search, initiated either through a tree structure or by means of keywords, causes the surfer to point to sites, pages or forums of which the title and/or content constitutes a violation of French law, as applies to the viewing of sites making an apology for Nazism and/or exhibiting uniforms, insignia or emblems resembling those worn or displayed by the Nazis,

or offering for sale objects or works whose sale is strictly prohibited in France, the surfer must desist from viewing the site concerned subject to imposition of the penalties provided in French legislation or the bringing of legal action against him.

Yahoo! challenged the French Court's competence to exert jurisdiction over the matter and claimed that there were no technical means available to prevent Internet users in France from having access to the offending pages. The Court addressed these arguments and upheld its earlier injunction in an opinion issued November 20, 2000.

LA LIGUE CONTRE LE RACISME ET L'ANTISEMITISME ("LICRA") AND L'UNION DES ETUDIANTS JUIFS DE FRANCE ("UEJF") v. YAHOO!, INC. AND YAHOO FRANCE

Interim Court Order, County Court of Paris, France, November 20, 2000.

Whereas in the opinion of the company YAHOO!, Inc.:

— this court is not competent to make a ruling in this dispute;

— there are no technical means capable of satisfying the terms of the order of 22nd May 2000;

— on the assumption that such means existed, their implementation would entail unduly high costs for the company, might even place the company in jeopardy and would to a degree compromise the existence of the Internet, being a space of liberty and scarcely receptive to attempts to control and restrict access;

Whereas in support of its incompetence plea, reiterated for the third time, the company YAHOO! points out that:

— its services are directed essentially at surfers located in the territory of the United States of America;

— its servers are installed in the same territory;

– a coercive measure instituted against it could have no application in the United States given that it would be in contravention of the first amendment of the United States Constitution which guarantees freedom of opinion and expression to every citizen;

Whereas it is true that the "Yahoo! Auctions" site is in general directed principally at surfers based in the United States having regard notably to the items posted for sale, the methods of payment envisaged, the terms of delivery, the language and the currency used, the same cannot be said to apply to the auctioning of objects representing symbols of Nazi ideology which may be of interest to any person;

Instead of challenging the Court's competence, could Yahoo! have argued, under conflicts of law principles, that the French court ought to apply U.S. law to its actions?

Whereas, furthermore, and as already ruled, the simple act of displaying such objects in France constitutes a violation of Article R645–1 of the Penal Code and therefore a threat to internal public order;

Whereas, in addition, this display clearly causes damage in France to the plaintiff associations who are justified in demanding the cessation and reparation thereof;

Whereas YAHOO! is aware that it is addressing French parties because upon making a connection to its auctions site from a terminal located in France it responds by transmitting advertising banners written in the French language;

Whereas a sufficient basis is thus established in this case for a connecting link with France, which renders our jurisdiction perfectly competent to rule in this matter;

Whereas any possible difficulties in executing our decision in the territory of the United States, as argued by YAHOO!, Inc., cannot by themselves justify a plea of incompetence;

Whereas this plea will therefore be rejected;

Whereas, on the argument developed by YAHOO! and based on the impossibility of implementing technical measures capable of satisfying the terms of the order of 22nd May 2000, it is necessary cite . . . the findings of the panel of consultants. . . .

Whereas it should be borne in mind that YAHOO!, Inc., already carries out geographical identification of French surfers or surfers operating out of French territory and visiting its auctions site, insofar as it routinely displays advertising banners in the French language targeted at these surfers, in respect of whom it therefore has means of identification; whereas YAHOO!, Inc., cannot properly maintain that this practice amounts to "crude technology" of limited reliability, unless it were felt that YAHOO!, Inc., had decided to spend money with no hope of a return or that it was deliberately misleading its advertisers about the quality of the services which it had undertaken to offer them, which does not appear to be so in this case;

Should potential difficulties in enforcement affect a court's decision whether to exercise jurisdiction? What is the point of the French court deciding the case if its judgment will be unenforceable?

Whereas in addition to the geographical identification as shown above to be already practised by YAHOO!, Inc., the consultants' report suggests that a request be made to surfers whose IP address is ambiguous (access through an anonymizer site—or allocation of IP addresses by AOL [or] COMPUSERVE which do not take account of the subscriber's country of origin) to provide a declaration of nationality, which in effect amounts to a declaration of the surfer's geographical origin, which YAHOO! could ask for when the home page is reached, or when a search is initiated for Nazi objects if the word "Nazi" appears in the user's search string, immediately before the request is processed by the search engine;

Whereas the consultants, who contest the arguments adduced by YAHOO!, Inc., as to the negative impact on such controls on the performance and response time of the server hosting the auctions site, estimate that a combination of two procedures, namely geographical identification and declaration of nationality, would enable a filtering success rate approaching 90 percent to be achieved; ...

Whereas, in addition to the measures suggested by the consultants, it is necessary to include checks by YAHOO! on the place of delivery of items purchased by auction;

Whereas, in effect, the act of visiting the auctions site for Nazi objects is not exclusively for the purpose of viewing; that this purpose is often to purchase items; that in these circumstances even if YAHOO! had been unable to identify with certainty the surfer's geographical origin, in this case France, it would know the place of delivery, and would be in a position to prevent the delivery from taking place if the delivery address was located in France; . . .

Whereas it adds that filtering of all information at Web server level would only be feasible if it were possible to ensure that the prohibition would only apply to French surfers, otherwise surfers throughout the world would be denied access to information published on its sites, which cannot be envisaged;

Whereas, however, it has been shown above that it does have effective filtering methods available to it; . . .

Whereas, according to the information given in the consultants' report at the initiative of the plaintiffs and which has not been seriously challenged, the company YAHOO! is currently refusing to accept through its auctions service the sale of human organs, drugs, works or objects connected with paedophilia, cigarettes or live animals, all such sales being automatically and justifiably excluded with the benefit of the first amendment of the American constitution guaranteeing freedom of opinion and expression;

What imperative is the court referring to here? Do you agree that such an imperative exists? Does it matter whether or not such an imperative exists?

Whereas it would most certainly cost the company very little to extend its ban to symbols of Nazism, and such an initiative would also have the merit of satisfying an ethical and moral imperative shared by all democratic societies; . . .

ON THESE GROUNDS

. . .

We reject the plea of incompetence reiterated by YAHOO!, Inc.;

We order YAHOO!, Inc., to comply within 3 months from notification of the present order with the injunctions contained in our order of 22nd May 2000 subject to a penalty of 100,000

Francs per day of delay effective from the first day following expiry of the 3 month period;

We instruct at the advanced cost of YAHOO!, Inc. . . . [a consultant] to undertake an assignment to prepare a consultancy report on the conditions of fulfilment of the terms of the aforementioned order; . . .

We find that YAHOO FRANCE has complied in large measure with the spirit and letter of the of the order of 22nd May 2000 containing an injunction against it;

We order it, however, to display a warning to surfers even before they have made use of the link to Yahoo.com, to be brought into effect within 2 months following notification of the present order;

We order YAHOO Inc. to pay to each of the plaintiffs the sum of 10,000 Francs pursuant to Article 700 of the New Code of Civil Procedure; . . .

We award costs to the charge of YAHOO Inc., with the exception of those arising from the petition brought against YAHOO! FRANCE which shall provisionally remain to the charge of each of the parties.

NOTES & QUESTIONS

1. Is this an example of a court attempting to exert unlimited jurisdiction over the Internet—that is, claiming the authority to enforce its sovereign's laws against all entities "on" the Internet? To what extent does the court ground its judgment on the presence of Yahoo! France within French borders, or the exposure to Yahoo!'s sites by French citizens or people on French territory?

2. Why is a "declaration of nationality" an acceptable means for Yahoo! to use to determine a user's geographic origin (especially in cases where the user has gone through an anonymizer

site)? Does the French court believe it is unlikely that users will lie? Does that matter? If not, why did it matter to the *ICraveTV* court?

3. Does it matter whether the site in controversy is yahoo.fr or yahoo.com?

BE CAREFUL WHAT YOU ASK FOR: RECONCILING A GLOBAL INTERNET AND LOCAL LAW (V)
Jonathan Zittrain
Who Rules the Net?, Cato Institute, 2003

The most intriguing developments in the running jurisdictional and governance debates have been those that point towards a reassertion of effective local government control over Internet usage of people within each government's territorial boundaries.

. . .

The French courts have indicated an awareness of the convoy problem in the suit brought against Yahoo! for permitting online auctions featuring the display of Nazi memorabilia in claimed contravention of local law. The outcome of that case so far has France asserting its right to demand that Yahoo! cease offering certain kinds of auctions, but only after the court chartered a three-expert panel to assess the extent to which Yahoo! could implement such a ban without having to apply it to non-French residents. [ ] The panel concluded that Yahoo! was in a position to more or less determine who was accessing its auctions from France and who was not, and therefore could apply the strictures of French law to French customers without depriving, say, Americans the opportunity to browse auctions of Nazi material. Firms have sprung up to offer just such geographic determinations, and while they are far from perfect, they can sort many users into territories, and require those who wish to evade the categorization to undertake some burden and inconvenience to mask their geo-identities. [ ]

Search engine Google, which offers country- and language-specific variants, apparently obeys the informal requests of officials from Germany to eliminate potentially illegal sites from its google.com counterpart at google.de. [ ] So far Germany does not appear to have asked Google to eliminate such sites from those presented to German-based visitors to google.com, but the notion of geographic-specific information tailoring has lodged.

Geolocation by online service providers is likely to become easier and more accurate over time. Global positioning system chips are decreasing in price and finding their ways into laptops, and commercial opportunities exist to offer services on the basis of geography—one might soon be able to step off a plane, open a laptop or handheld personal digital assistant, and find an ad for local restaurants with automatic delivery displayed on the first sponsored Web site one visits. To the extent geolocation is possible, the convoy problem described earlier in this chapter begins to melt away. Purveyors of information may object to the administrative burden of having to tailor information for multiple jurisdictions—just as opponents of nationwide collection of local state sales taxes in the U.S. point to the difficulties of mastering each state's sales tax collection and remittance rules—but that complaint is much less searing and separate from the objection that one jurisdiction's residents will be de facto subject to another's laws because of a Web site's all-or-nothing exposure to the Net's masses.

Many old-school Netizens, eager to maintain a global Internet unsusceptible to government control, were furious at their technologically savvy brethren for adverting to the possibility of geolocation in the Yahoo! France case. This led to some perhaps-chastened repudiation of the court's decision by at least two members of the panel that enabled it, Internet pioneers Ben Laurie and Vint Cerf. Laurie outright apologized, and Cerf was quoted after the decision as making the observation "that if every jurisdiction in the world insisted on some form of filtering for its particular geographic territory, the World Wide Web would stop functioning." [ ] That's an overstatement in the sense that sources of content on the Web are perfectly able to tailor their information delivery on the basis of whatever demographic they can solicit or discern from those who surf their Web sites. But it is completely accurate if one believes in "World Wide" as an affirmative ideological value for the Internet, rather than a technical description of its historically undifferentiated reach.

One can imagine a framework for Internet content providers—whether large Web site operators or individual home page designers or message board posters—where prior to information going public, a set of checkboxes is presented where the publisher can indicate just where in the world the information is to be exposed. One could check or uncheck "United States" as a whole, or select specific states. One could check or uncheck Zimbabwe, or Australia, or the European Union. Such technological flexibility, combined with varied demands by countries for providers to filter content to hew to local laws, might induce risk-averse Internet content providers to adopt a very narrow band of publishing for their work—generally asking to limit distribution to those areas where legal risk is deemed low, or at least where potential profit from the work's consumption there is thought to exceed such risk. [footnote omitted] Users eager for information will then be effectively denied access to it by faraway content providers anticipating the actions of zealous local governments seeking to expand their local regulation of more traditional media into the formerly unregulable Internet space. Worse, overcautious or simply indifferent Internet content providers will omit "unimportant" countries from the list of places able to view their offerings, enhancing a digital divide even though such countries are not explicitly seeking strong control over Internet content. Indeed, the gleam of the World Wide Web would be dulled as it became simply another window into traditional content for many surfers, rather than a raucous digital free-for-all.

Such a scenario is not inevitable, however. Countries worried about being left off information providers' checkbox list could pass safe harbor legislation providing for immunity as an enticement to content providers to allow them to remain on the list of digital destinations. Or they might index their laws to those of countries that will rarely be omitted from checkbox lists—just as Sealand's ban on the hosting of child pornography is a one sentence pointer to whatever the United States has legislated on the issue. The search for "global law" might be given a strong push as countries seek to be clumped together in the minds of content providers.

Yahoo! and Democracy on the Internet
Joel R. Reidenberg
42 Jurimetrics J. 261 (2002)

"Internet separatists" believe that the Net is a separate jurisdiction that transcends national borders and the control of nation–states. They reject the complex relationship between the network and physical territory. They favor allowing Internet actors to determine their own rules, and they reject the capability of democratic states to regulate behavior on the Internet. The Separatist philosophy derives largely from the American value placed on the unfettered flow of information, a value that is embedded in the present architecture of the Internet through the geographic indeterminacy of Internet transmissions.

The *Yahoo!* decision, however, represents an affirmation of non–U.S. democratic values and comes at a critical developmental juncture for the Internet. The French democracy has chosen rules for free expression in its criminal code that are consistent with international human rights but that do not mirror the U.S. constitutional protections found in the First Amendment. The Internet gives neither policy a greater claim to legitimacy than the other. Yet, *Yahoo!* reflects a shifting economic and political power struggle on the Internet that suggests that the American position is becoming a minority view.

. . .

The normative impact of *Yahoo!* is that Internet actors will have to recognize varying public values across national borders. The decision begins to force the technical elites to respect democratically chosen values and the rule of law. The architecture that makes geographic filtering difficult is not immutable. Ironically, economic actors have been promoting technologies of localization and identification for commercial gain, such as intellectual property rights management and enforcement and the development of marketing profiles. . . .

I. The Enforcement of French Law Within French Territory

While the Internet enables actors to reach a geographically dispersed audience, the Internet does not change the accountability of those actors for their conduct within national borders. Similarly, the Internet does not vitiate the responsibility and the power of states to police activities within their territories. Aside from a few Internet separatists, no one could seriously challenge that France has jurisdiction to prescribe rules for activities within French territory. Yahoo!, however, thought it was above the law in places where it did business on the Internet because it operated from U.S.-based servers.

. . .

On the surface, the *Yahoo!* case is a mundane exercise in the analysis of territorial sovereignty and personal jurisdiction. The American company sought to have a worldwide presence and maintained extensive contacts and business relationships in France. The Web pages at issue, though based in the United States, were expressly designed to reach a global audience. In this context, one could hardly imagine a national court refusing to exercise personal jurisdiction and refusing to apply the local law against a company seeking to conduct business in its territory. . . .

A. An Inevitable Result

. . .

Yahoo! argued that its actions were committed in the United States and therefore beyond French territorial jurisdiction. Yahoo asserted that the physical situs of its servers in the United States rather than the transmission and display in France of Nazi material determined the "localization" of Yahoo!'s activity. The Internet does not, however, displace the well-established principle in international law that allows states to exercise prescriptive jurisdiction for conduct having effects occurring within the national territory. The intentional transmission by Yahoo! of communications from servers in the United States to France brings the conduct within the prescriptive jurisdiction of France, and the French court noted that the "visualization" of Nazi objects in France was a violation of the French law; the display on a computer screen takes place in France and satisfies the requirement of having an element of the infraction occur within France.

When Yahoo! manifestly refused to comply with the original injunction of the French court, the company expected the American First Amendment to apply to its global activities. Under U.S. law, there is no doubt that Yahoo! had a legal right to express reprehensible ideas and policies within the United States. But this right is a national right and does not extend extraterritorially beyond the U.S. border. The American right does not apply to the dissemination of Web pages in France to French Web users.

With respect to the competence of foreign courts to judge Yahoo!'s actions launched from California servers, Yahoo!'s extensive efforts to reach foreign users from the United States gives foreign countries the power to adjudicate the company's activities. . . .

. . .

Because Yahoo targeted French users with advertisements in French, the company could not seriously contend that it sought only to reach an American audience with the U.S.-based Web services and that Yahoo! did not intend to profit from French Web surfers. . . .

B. Similar Internet Sovereignty Decisions in American Courts

The French court's exercise of sovereignty has support in the decisions of American courts. The United States has long faced the problem of territorial jurisdiction and choice of law in disputes involving parties in different states. The Constitution requires that the exercise of a state court's territorial jurisdiction be reasonable and fair to the defendant. The basic test is whether the foreign party engaged in "purposeful activity" with the forum state. To the extent that a foreign party purposefully availed itself of the opportunities in the forum, then the forum can judge the conduct of the foreign party. Courts must assess the factual situation to make this determination.

The Internet does not change the principle, but the courts have struggled to determine if an Internet site actively sought to target the forum state. . . .

. . .The cases reveal that, to the extent that an Internet actor strives to target users in a foreign jurisdiction, the foreign forum can assert territorial jurisdiction and apply the forum's law . . . . Courts assert territorial jurisdiction to protect values held in the forum. In this context, the French decision is an ordinary exercise of a widely accepted practice in the United States. A U.S. court faced with the same facts would yield a similar result.

. . .

II. The Democratizing Impact on Internet Architecture

. . .

A. Public Values Embedded in Internet Architecture

Yahoo! shows clearly how certain public values are embedded in the current Internet architecture. Yahoo!, in essence, sought refuge in the Internet's technical protocol to obtain immunity for its worldwide behavior. Yahoo! argued that it could not filter out French Web users because of the geographic indeterminacy of data transmissions on the Internet. This defense highlights the extent to which technological choices have established information policy rules.

These key technological rules have, however, been heavily influenced by American and Internet Separatist values. In particular, as Yahoo! tried to assert, the First Amendment plays an important role in the current Internet architecture. The modern First Amendment jurisprudence establishes a standard of an unfettered flow of information as the basic rule. Internet separatists similarly argue that "information wants to be free."

. . .

The U.S. cultural value of the free flow of information is embedded in the technical rules of data transmission over the Internet. Current Internet architecture seeks to make distance and geographic location irrelevant for the transmission of information. Data transmissions depend on a technique called "packet switching" and the use of numeric addresses known as "Internet Protocol" (IP) addresses. These numbers, much like a telephone number, enable the switching of bits of data from one point on the Internet to another. Under the transmission control protocol, any single message may be divided into multiple packets of data, and each packet of data travels a different path to reach the destination where the message is reassembled. The effect of this design is to minimize borders and barriers to the free flow of information on the Internet. This philosophy matches the American belief in information freedom and the Internet Separatist view of the global network.

Nevertheless, these embedded rules do not reflect more subtle policies of information freedoms found in other democracies and in international human rights law. As the French ruling illustrates, other democracies give more weight to other fundamental human rights and interests, including racial, ethnic and religious freedoms, privacy and reputation, when those rights and interests conflict with free speech.

. . .

To Yahoo! and the Internet separatists, the embedding of public values in the technical infrastructure assures that the United States' architectural philosophy and free market bias will prevail over all other architectural choices. Yet, it is wishful thinking to assume that geographic indeterminacy will prevail and that the Internet is pure information. Regulation and market pressures are already changing the Internet. Intellectual property right holders have insisted on enlarging their legal and public rights to exclude others from information, and commercial models are driving the move toward user localization for product customization and marketing. The code is not static. . . .

B. The Empowerment of States to Protect Local Values

The *Yahoo!* case has valuable implications for democratizing technological development and advancing democratic pluralism on the Internet. Until now, Internet separatists have had a relatively free rein to define the infrastructure rules, and the technological choices reflected U.S.–centric norms. Yahoo challenged the legitimacy of foreign public law when the company argued that the geographic indeterminacy of Web–based data transmission should provide immunity for the company's worldwide behavior. The French rejection of this position shows that Internet companies cannot supplant the rule of law as established by elected representatives. This position promotes democratic pluralism on the Internet by requiring technological developments that allow states to enforce their local laws.

France has forced the recognition of French public values in dealing with French Web users. At a time when Neo–Nazi Web sites flock to the United States to benefit from the constitutional protection accorded to hate–mongering, this determination of liability enables France to preserve its democratically chosen public order law.

Public accountability under national law rejects the Internet separatists' view that technologists should determine the network rules for democratic society. As technical rules are not immutable, local liability gives states a voice in the embedded values of the Internet architecture. *Yahoo!* forces technological recognition of democratically adopted laws.

National liability for local conduct obligates a form of policy zoning for the Internet that allows states to protect their values in their own territories. Under the *Yahoo!* decision, Internet companies will be required to make structural changes in their system architecture. France has called for geographic determinism on the Internet and has overturned the technologists' decision to embed the political value of geographic ambiguity for the origin of Internet data transmissions. . . .

. . .

In contrast to the enforcement problems created by the Internet's locational ambiguity, geographic identification empowers states to implement a variety of public policies within their territories, including the enforcement of intellectual property rights, consumer protection, and data privacy through geographic filtering. The alternative, the incapacity of states to enforce such regulations on the Internet, vitiates the basic ideal of democratic society—allowing citizens to choose their governing rules.

NOTES & QUESTIONS

1. Compare Reidenberg's contention that "the incapacity of states to enforce such regulations on the Internet, vitiates the basic ideal of democratic society—allowing citizens to choose their governing rules" with the Ninth Circuit's observation that "Yahoo! cannot expect both to benefit from the fact that its content may be viewed around the world and to be shielded from the resulting costs—one of which is that, if Yahoo! violates the speech laws of another nation, it must wait for the foreign litigants to come to the United States to enforce the judgment before its First Amendment claim may be heard by a U.S. court." *Yahoo! Inc. v. La Ligue Contre le Racisme et l'Antisemitisme,* 379 F.3d 1120, 1126 (9th Cir. 2004).

2. One alternative to a country exercising jurisdiction over foreign companies operating online is to simply change the architecture of the Internet within its borders so as to enable government censorship. Is that an appropriate alternative? Is that a solution to the *Yahoo! France* case? If we say that jurisdiction is inappropriate in a given situation, are we compelled to say that a government's only alternative is to modify the code underlying its nation's Internet access? For a growing catalogue of the filtering and surveillance activities of countries, see the OpenNet Initiative at http://www.opennetinitiative.net/.

IV. Conclusion

The Internet of tomorrow may not look much like the Internet of today. Some of the activities most objectionable to regulators—such as file sharing—may be curtailed through a variety of interventions entailing cooperation across governments and a spectrum of private sector entities. Modifications to Internet architecture to permit Internet activities to be associated with their originating physical regions may ultimately create a series of Internets and Internet experiences—ones modulated by various sovereigns' regulatory visions.

Be Careful What You Ask For: Reconciling a Global Internet and Local Law (VI)
Jonathan Zittrain
Who Rules the Net?, Cato Institute, 2003

> . . . [I]nformation is an atomic unit of a free society . . . . [A] medium [such as the Internet] that permits such extraordinary information access and manipulation by individuals so effortlessly across distances—as speakers, browsers, searchers, and consumers—is one that can be more than a new way of shopping, checking the weather, or watching traditional television at user–selected times.
>
> As the Internet becomes part of daily living rather than a place to visit, its rough edges are smoothed and its extremes tamed by sovereigns wanting to protect consumers, prevent network resource abuse, and eliminate speech deemed harm-

ful. The tools are now within reach to permit sovereigns with competing rulesets to play down their differences—whether by countenancing global privatization of some Internet governance issues through organizations like ICANN, coming to new international agreements on substance and procedure to reduce the friction caused by transborder data flows, or by a live and let live set of localization technologies to shape the Internet to suit the respective societies it touches.

Would changing Internet architecture to allow sovereigns to enforce their laws upon their own citizens be a good idea or a bad one?

What we might gain in easing jurisdictional tensions we could stand to lose in revolutionary capacity. The point of inflection at which the World Wide Internet sits asks us to choose which we value more—international harmony and diversity that includes censorship smacking of repression, or an unavoidable baseline of freedom of expression that permits harmful speech along with constructive speech. Can those who wish for civil liberty without child pornography and rampant copyright infringement have it both ways?

[As] Barlow wrote: We cannot separate the air that chokes from the air upon which wings beat. [ ] But governments are likely to try. The battles to watch, then, are not abstruse jurisdictional ones that [are] . . . more or less settled or stale whether on or off the Internet, but rather the dueling trajectories by which we embrace the Internet's freedom and curse its anarchy, love its instantaneous, global scope and regret the refuge it offers to those who lie, cheat, and steal at a distance.

INDEX

References are to Pages.

113

†